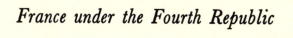

France under the Fourth Republic

FRANCE

under the Fourth Republic

FRANÇOIS GOGUEL

NEW YORK / RUSSELL & RUSSELL

Foreword

THIS volume is the third of a series devoted to the political, economic, and constitutional problems of postwar France and Italy. The series is part of a "French-Italian Inquiry" undertaken at Cornell University in 1949 in the belief that the changes brought about by fascism, revolution, and war in these two key countries of Western Europe were sufficiently significant to warrant study.

The two first volumes have dealt with two of the more far-reaching political ideologies of today, communism and Christian Democracy.[1]

The present volume focuses our attention on the most meaningful effort to reconstruct parliamentary government in postwar Europe. Under the guidance of François Goguel, the reader will follow the vicissitudes of the first five years of the Fourth Republic. This is above all an inquiry into the operation of the party system in France within the framework of the new constitution of 1946. But it offers us as well in Chapter V a perceptive analysis of the fundamental difficulties of French society and of the French system of government. It should provide the American reader with a satisfying guide to the complexities of French life, at a moment when the overcoming of the recriminations and misunderstand-

---

[1] Mario Einaudi, Jean-Marie Domenach, Aldo Garosci, *Communism in Western Europe* (Ithaca, N.Y.: Cornell University Press, 1951); Mario Einaudi and François Goguel, *Christian Democracy in Italy and France* (Notre Dame, Ind.: University of Notre Dame Press, 1952).

v

ings that have afflicted American-French relationships in recent years is more important than ever.

François Goguel no longer needs any introduction to the American public. As the author of many works and essays on French political life he has acquired an outstanding position among the younger generation of French scholars.

The Inquiry has been made possible by a Rockefeller grant to Cornell University. I am greatly indebted to Ina Loewenberg for her assistance and to Roy Pierce of Smith College for his skillful translation of the French manuscript.

MARIO EINAUDI

Cornell University
June 1952

Contents

	Foreword	v
	Introduction	ix
I	The Political Evolution of the First National Assembly	1
	The Beginnings of the Fourth Republic	1
	The End of Tripartism: January–October 1947	20
	The Attempt to Form a Third Force: November 1947	33
	The Enlarged Third Force: November 1947–June 1951	37
	The Transformation of the RPF into a Party: November 1947–June 1951	47
II	The Electoral Reform of 1951	58
	The Electoral System after the Liberation	58
	The Early Criticisms of Proportional Representation	62
	The Problem of Electoral Reform: 1950–1951	66
	The Electoral Law of May 9, 1951	73
III	The Elections of June 17, 1951	79
	The Electoral Campaign and the Alliances	80
	The Electoral Returns	90
	The Strength of the Parties in the Assembly	117
IV	Party Conflicts in the New National Assembly	121
	The Areas of Discord among the Center Parties	122
	The Difficulties in Electing a Premier	129
	The Dislocation of the Center Majority Caused by the Passage of the Educational Laws	133

V   The Fundamental Problems of French Political
       Life   137

   Causes and Characteristics of the Party Struggle   137
   The Problem of Institutions   146
   The Problem of the Majority   171

   Epilogue   183

   The Formation and Success of the Pinay Government   183
   The Significance of Pinay's Success   187
   The Prospects for the Future   189

   Index   193

Introduction

This study, undertaken initially as an analysis of the political situation in France after the elections of June 17, 1951, quite naturally turned into an account and an appraisal of the first five years of the Fourth Republic. It is impossible to understand the meaning of the elections of 1951 without a knowledge of the electoral law which was adopted a few weeks before the elections and of the circumstances in which the parties entered the electoral contest. That law and those circumstances are direct products of the political evolution of France since 1946.

There should be no need to say that this account of the first five years of the Fourth Republic does not pretend to be, in the exact sense of the word, a *history*, something that it is obviously much too soon to undertake. Moreover, the appraisal can only be provisional, for the data upon which it is based are continually being modified. But the French political situation has been so profoundly transformed in the last six years that it is not without value to try to examine the changes which have taken place, to investigate their causes, and to survey the prospects which they seem to offer for the future. These are the objects of this study.

One might be tempted to think, at first glance, that after the great, but artificial, upheavals caused by the Second World War, by the existence of the Vichy government, and by the Liberation, French political life between 1946 and 1951 merely tended to return, by a sort of pendulous movement, to its former behavior patterns. With respect to institutions, a number of innovations introduced into the constitution of October 27, 1946, have been altered in practice, sometimes to the point where they have been tacitly abrogated. This has been the case, in particular, with the procedures adopted by the framers of the constitution in order to establish the political responsibility of the cabinet before the National Assembly. It had been hoped, in 1946, that ministerial stability would be guaranteed by permitting the posing of a question of confidence only after a special deliberation of the Council of Ministers, by requiring an interval of one full day between the posing of the question of confidence and the vote upon it, and by requiring an absolute majority of the members of the National Assembly for a refusal of confidence. Of the eleven ministerial crises which occurred between January 1946 and June 1952, however, only two—those which brought about the resignations of the Bidault cabinet in June 1950 and of the Pleven cabinet in January 1952—took place in the circumstances envisaged by the drafters of the constitution. The nine other crises were caused, just as crises were caused during the Third Republic, either by the internal disintegration of a coalition government or by a hostile vote passed by a simple majority in the National Assembly, without any question of confidence having been posed "in the constitutional forms." Usage very quickly demonstrated that a Premier could pose a question of confidence in fact without having to pose it legally.

Furthermore, the Council of the Republic, whose members adopted the title of senator at the end of 1948, and whose method of election since then has closely approximated that of the Senate of the Third Republic, has not been able to reconquer for itself the important political and legislative powers of the former upper chamber. However, it demands them perseveringly, and the prospect is that a constitutional amendment will one day create for the second chamber a more important role in the Fourth Republic than the one which was so grudgingly conceded to it in 1946. On the other hand, neither the Assembly of the French Union nor the Economic Council—both established in 1946—is playing the important role that the constitution makers had anticipated. The Council of the Republic outweighs them by far in political prestige; for proof of this, one has only to observe the large number of their members who present themselves as candidates in senatorial elections.

Experience reveals, therefore, that the structure and effective operation of the institutions of the Fourth Republic are infinitely more similar to the usages of the Third Republic than an examination of the constitution of 1946 and a consideration of the state of mind of the drafters of the constitution would lead one to expect.

A similar conclusion might be drawn from a consideration of the alliances between parties and the composition of governing coalitions. In 1946, Communists, Socialists, and Christian Democrats were united in a tripartite majority, against which the Moderates and the Radicals, who had formerly been irreconcilable adversaries, were united in a common opposition. In the spring of 1947, however, tripartism was shattered by the elimination of the Communists from the government, and the majority was enlarged toward the Center when a certain number of Radicals and even Moderates joined forces with the Christian Democrats and the Socialists.

At the same time, the formation by General de Gaulle of the Rassemblement du Peuple Français (RPF, Rally of the French People), and the crystallization around it of an opposition hostile to the fundamental principles of the constitutional system of 1946, forced this new Center majority to contend on two fronts simultaneously: against an extreme Left opposition, that of the Communists; and against a Right opposition, that of the Gaullist opponents of the regime. In many respects, this situation recalled others which had occurred several times during the Third Republic. The movement of the Socialists into the opposition after the elections of June 17, 1951, and the formation of the Moderate and conservative majority in support of the Pinay government—a majority joined by a certain number of dissidents from the RPF—also call to mind several precedents: that of the Méline majority of 1896–1898, that of the Bloc National of 1919–1924, and that of the Moderate Chamber of 1928–1932.

This double evolution of institutions and of political attitudes might lead one to believe that no fundamental changes have occurred since 1939 in the basic facts of French political life and that, after an apparent upheaval, things are tending once again to resume their normal course. When carefully considered, however, it appears that such a conclusion would be superficial and inexact.

The nature of the RPF opposition, interested both in governmental effectiveness and in social progress, differs markedly from that of the antiparliamentary right-wing groups of the Third Republic. The creation, the development, and the consolidation of a large Christian Democratic party, the Mouvement Républicain Populaire (MRP, Popular Republican Movement), which is closer in many respects to socialism than it is to the Moderates, constitutes an entirely new fact, and all its consequences upon French political life have undoubtedly not yet become apparent. The movement of the Radicals to an increasingly frank position of conservatism is no less important. Several basic factors of the French political problem have, therefore, changed since the prewar period; they have changed decisively and, it would appear, permanently.

As far as institutions are concerned, if it is true that custom has led them into the pattern of the Third Republic, it is also highly unlikely that they can endure for long in their present form. Governmental instability, the incoherence (due largely to the defects of the electoral system) of the majorities which are formed, the slowness and inefficiency of parliamentary procedures—all call for basic reforms. It is the merit of the RPF that it has defined these reforms, although it is also true that the RPF has rendered their accomplishment difficult by its intransigent tactics and the tactlessness of some of its slogans. But whether it is accomplished with the RPF or without it, it seems inevitable that a basic constitutional revision will take place during the coming months; the necessity for this revision is becoming increasingly clear. It is precisely because the constitution makers of 1946 did not succeed in correcting the faults of the constitutional laws of 1875 that their work must, sooner or later, be undertaken once again.

The changes that have taken place in the constellation of political parties, as well as those which are bound to take place in the institutional sphere, all stem from the enormous transformations which are occurring in the economic structure of France. Deprived of the wealth from its foreign investments and of many of its productive facilities, the French economy was badly damaged at the end of the Second World War. Economic recovery, the re-establishment of a viable system of internal exchange and foreign trade, required an immense effort toward modernization, which was undertaken under the auspices of the Monnet Plan and accomplished, to a large extent, thanks to Marshall Plan aid. This modernization program is transforming the industrial, agricultural, and social structure of the country. The French crisis in the political sphere at least partially reflects the difficulties of this transition period, which has not yet terminated.

The economic and social changes which have already taken place or which are in the process of coming about—like the change in the international situation since the prewar period—are too vast for it to be possible, on the political level, seriously to entertain the hypothesis of a pure and simple return to the traditions of the Third Republic. The Fourth Republic has undoubtedly not yet revealed its permanent distinguishing characteristics: the tableau of the first five years of its existence will demonstrate this clearly. But it appears to be completely out of the question that the transition period, of which this book attempts to clarify the major political aspects, can be concluded with a mere return to the *status quo ante bellum.*

FRANÇOIS GOGUEL

Middlebury College
June 1952

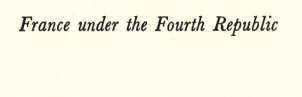

France under the Fourth Republic

I

The Political Evolution of the First National Assembly

THE National Assembly elected on November 10, 1946, after the promulgation of the constitution which had been ratified by the voters at the referendum of October 13, seemed to come into existence under the aegis of tripartism, the governmental alliance of the Communist party, the Socialist party and the Popular Republican Movement (MRP). With the single exception of one Radical, Alexander Varenne, who had belonged to the Socialist party during most of his political career under the Third Republic and who had entered the government personally, without committing his group, the Bidault cabinet, which was in power for the duration of the Second Constituent Assembly, from June to November 1946, consisted only of Communists, Socialists, and Popular Republicans, and it was a majority composed of these three parties which had adopted the constitution that was presented at the referendum of October 13.

The Beginnings of the Fourth Republic

This coalition of Communists, Socialists, and Christian Democrats differed in every respect from the political traditions of the Third Republic. It was distinctive, first of all, because of its size, as it was supported by almost three-fourths of the members of the

Assembly, while the parliamentary majorities of the Third Republic had usually been much smaller. It was distinctive because of its form, as it was a coalition of three highly organized parties capable of maintaining rigid discipline among their representatives in Parliament, while the Third Republic had been characterized by extreme individualism and the attitudes of individual men had usually been more important than those of the parties. It was distinctive, finally, because of its composition, for it consisted of two parties claiming to embody the traditions of the Left, and even of the extreme Left, and a Christian Democratic group whose principal support came from regions and social groups that were traditionally conservative.

Moreover, tripartism cast together in a joint opposition the Catholic Moderates and the free-thinking, anticlerical Radicals, while the essential element of political life during the Third Republic had been the rivalry of these two groups. They had always opposed each other at election time even when the Radicals, unable to reach agreement with their Socialist allies on a governmental program, resigned themselves temporarily to sharing power with the Catholic Moderates. The formation of a political coalition so foreign to French political tradition can be explained only in terms of the consequences of the war and of the Resistance.

The old "moderate" [conservative] and Catholic parties which had, during the last twenty years of the Third Republic, constantly enjoyed the support of a bit less than or—in 1919 and 1928—a bit more than half the voters and which had wielded or shared power during fourteen of these twenty years, were discredited after the Liberation by the support that many of their leaders had given to the Vichy government. The Radicals were weakened for the same reason and also because they had long been considered as the embodiment of the spirit and the methods of the Third Republic. At the end of the war a large sector of the public wanted to abandon the old political habits which, rightly or wrongly, it held responsible for the disasters of 1940. This explains why the two political groups which, sometimes separately and sometimes together (in what were called governments of National Union, created after the collapse of Left and extreme Left majorities), had always wielded power under the Third Republic were so weakened after the Liberation that they could simply be disregarded. But why, on the other hand, were the proponents of tripartism so powerful, and what were the factors drawing them together?

The MRP was not France's first Christian Democratic party, but its predecessors during the Third Republic, the Popular Democratic party and the League of the Young Republic, had never succeeded in winning many Catholics away from the conservative and moderate parties. The discredit which struck the old Right after the war, however, liberated the bulk of its previous electoral support and enabled the Popular Republicans to win most of it for themselves. The hostility toward Vichy of the leaders of the new movement, their participation in the Resistance, and the good relations that General de Gaulle was supposed to have with them seemed to guarantee them a major role in the political life of liberated France. Many conservative voters gave them their support, in spite of the MRP's far-from-conservative economic and social program, in the hope that they would be able to oppose effectively any revolutionary activities that the Communists might undertake. It was largely because of their supposed understanding with General de Gaulle and, especially, of the desire to strengthen the most effective of the noncommunist parties that many citizens of conservative tendencies gave the Popular Republicans their votes after October 1945.

The Socialist party, although it had been in power from 1936 to 1938 and was therefore open to attack on the grounds of sharing in the responsibility for the defeat of 1940, and although a number of its representatives in the National Assembly had voted to delegate power to Pétain in July 1940 and could therefore be accused of having compromised with the antirepublican and defeatist Vichy government, did not suffer the same discredit as the Moderates and the Radicals. The part played in the Resistance by many Socialist party leaders, as well as Léon Blum's courageous attitude at the trial Pétain brought against him and his deportation to Germany, had erased the memory of the acts for which certain of its members could be reproached. Moreover, after the Liberation, the reconstituted Socialist party had pitilessly banished from its ranks everyone who had in any way compromised with the Vichy regime. It had participated very loyally in the provisional government of General de Gaulle. Its ideology and its program had much in common with those elaborated in secrecy by the movements of the Resistance, aiming at the political, economic, and social reorganization of the country after the Liberation. All this had enabled it in the elections of 1945 to win back and even to increase its electoral strength of 1936. It is true that it lost some of its old working-class support to the Communists, but it gained, on the other hand, in the old rural fiefs of the Radicals.

The great increase in the strength of communism after the Liberation may appear at first sight to be more surprising than the growth of Christian Democracy and the maintenance by the Socialists of their former position. Beginning with the German-Soviet pact of 1939 and especially after the entrance of Russian troops into Poland at the end of September, the Communist party had adopted an attitude of revolutionary defeatism. After the Armistice of June 1940 its clandestine propaganda had opposed the Gaullist Resistance. Some of its leaders, although imprisoned by the Vichy government, asked to be heard as witnesses for the prosecution at the Riom trial brought by Pétain against Léon Blum, Paul Reynaud, and Edouard Daladier. After the outbreak of hostilities between Nazi Germany and the USSR, however, the French Communists put their secret organization and the unlimited devotion of their militants at the service of the Resistance against the occupation forces and the Vichy government. They soon acknowledged the authority of General de Gaulle, although they jealously preserved the autonomy of their military formations and intelligence organization. The noncommunist elements in the Resistance, who wanted to form as united a movement as possible of all the forces which might contribute to the Liberation of the country, overlooked the attitude that their new comrades had held from August 1939 to June 1941. The Communists were given places in the leading organizations of the Resistance: in the Committee of National Liberation at Algiers and in the National Council of the Resistance in occupied France.

The large role played by the Communists in the course of the war and the influence of the *maquis* controlled by their organization of Franc-Tireurs et Partisans would have been enough in themselves to make the Communist party more important after the Liberation than it had been before the war. But the absurd propaganda of the Vichy government which, in order to discredit the Resistance, continually denounced it as being entirely inspired and dominated by the Communists, undoubtedly aided the Communists as effectively as did the role that they actually took in the struggle. This propaganda, instead of discrediting the Resistance, helped the Communist party win the support of many people who began to consider it a national party. The desire for basic social changes, which was particularly widespread among the young people who grew to manhood during the occupation as well as among the working classes, whose suffering had been great from 1940 to 1944, also contributed, as did the prestige of Soviet Russia, to the growth of communism. In the elections of October 1945 the Communist party, which had been able to win only 15.5 per cent of the votes in 1936, won 26.5 per cent of the votes and became the largest party in France.

As to the collaboration between Popular Republicans, Socialists, and Communists in the government, this was also made possible and undoubtedly even inevitable by the circumstances of the Resistance and the occupation.

The principal concern of General de Gaulle and his delegates in occupied France, especially Jean Moulin, had been to unite in the Resistance and in its representative organs qualified members of every shade of public opinion, representatives of all the spiritual currents and of all the social classes of the country. This is why the Committee of National Liberation, which was at first composed of military men, civil servants, and men without any past political experience, was gradually opened to representatives of political parties, including the Communist party, while Jean Moulin persuaded the representatives of the Resistance movements to accept representatives of the political parties and trade unions in the National Council of the Resistance as well. The dissolution of the Third International facilitated the reconciliation of the other groups with the Communist party, as it seemed to guarantee the party's purely national character. In addition, the real solidarity that was created among the resistants of all political beliefs by the dangers they faced together in the underground struggle, and the personal contacts created by this solidarity, were important factors in the reconciliation of parties which had formerly been opposed to one another. It seems quite natural also that the provisional government formed on French soil by General de Gaulle after the Liberation of Paris should have been what Léon Blum had called in 1938 a government of "national unanimity," extending from certain Moderates who had taken part in the Resistance to the Communists.

This was precisely the political formula followed by General de Gaulle when he formed his cabinet in November 1945, after the election of the First Constituent Assembly. From this moment on, however, it became apparent that national unanimity was no more than a fiction. Many Moderates feared that the grip of the Communists and the Socialists on the government and the Assembly would produce truly revolutionary changes—both in the political system and in the economic structure—which they could not support. The majority of the Radicals shared these fears and were suspicious of General de Gaulle's tendencies to exercise power personally. The Communists, who had more or less slyly opposed De Gaulle since the fall of 1944, although they were represented in the provisional government, wanted to maneuver in such a way as to assure themselves of a decisive influence in the Assembly and in the government, which implied an intention sooner or later to eliminate De Gaulle, whose personal authority might be the major obstacle to their eventual attempts to assume power. Only the Popular Republicans and the Socialists seemed to be genuinely in favor of maintaining the governmental formula created in 1944, that is, the collaboration of all the parties under the leadership of General de Gaulle. The Popular Republicans saw this as a guarantee against the expansion of Communist influence. The Socialists saw it as a way of reconciling on the one hand the sentiments of many of their militants who, for doctrinal and traditional reasons, were in favor of "working-class unity," which meant close agreement with the Communists, and on the other hand the fear of their most experienced leaders, especially Léon Blum, that the Communists would win a decisive victory over the Socialists if the latter allowed themselves to be driven into a government of the extreme Left.

General de Gaulle's temperament made him unable to lead a coalition government. Instead of mediating among the parties and suggesting compromises to them, he tried constantly to impose his own views on them. He discovered very quickly that they would not accept these views, especially on the constitutional question, and he brusquely resigned on January 20, 1946. The political crisis which followed had a decisive influence on subsequent developments and is worth examination.

In his letter of resignation [1] the General explained that his departure was based on the conviction he had long held that his task "should end when the representatives of the nation were reassembled and when the political parties would be in a position to assume their responsibilities." He said that he had agreed to remain in power after the election of the Constituent Assembly only "in order to facilitate a necessary transition" and stated that "this transition is now accomplished." The last statement had no basis in fact. Having sat for hardly two months, the Assembly had been able neither to draft a constitution nor to define an economic, social, and financial policy capable of ensuring the recovery of the country. General de Gaulle's departure, in spite of

[1] *L'Année Politique 1946,* p. 529.

the difficulties which had arisen between him and certain parties of the majority, certainly was hardly likely to help the Assembly accomplish its tasks.

It seems that the real reason for the General's resignation was the desire to force the parties to pay greater heed to his wishes than they had been disposed to until that time. He undoubtedly thought that if he resigned, the Constituent Assembly, divided into several parties which were clearly antagonistic to one another, would be incapable of electing a new Provisional President, and he hoped that after an indefinite period of impotence it would be forced to make a new appeal to him. Then he would be in a position to impose his views on the parties. This reasoning was based on some unverifiable hypotheses of political psychology, and it ignored one unquestionable arithmetical fact. Within the Constituent Assembly there was an extreme Left majority composed of 151 Communists, 8 crypto-Communists, and 147 Socialists, making a total of 306 deputies out of 586. The General's tactics assumed however that an important part of the Assembly—and De Gaulle probably counted on the MRP here—would try to bring about the old Provisional President's return to power.

The leaders of the MRP did not share the opinion that was undoubtedly held by De Gaulle that the formation of an extreme Left majority, of which the Communists might soon become the almost complete masters, was politically inconceivable although arithmetically possible. They were aware of the strength among the Socialist militants of the traditions of working-class unity, and they believed it to be indispensable, in order to prevent any extension of the Communist party's grip on the state, to help the Socialists to avoid a forced collaboration exclusively with the Communists. This seems to be the only explanation of why, three days after General de Gaulle's resignation, the representatives of the MRP reached an agreement with the Socialist and Communist parties on the program for a tripartite government, to be presided over by a Socialist, Félix Gouin, who was then president of the Constituent Assembly.

This decision, in conformity with the democratic tradition which holds that there is no such thing as an indispensable man and which requires the uninterrupted operation of parliamentary institutions, precluded the possibility of General de Gaulle's returning to power in the near future. It seems that De Gaulle never forgave the leaders of the MRP for this, as two months earlier they had proclaimed that the MRP was "the party of fidelity." On the other hand, the most elementary political prudence should have led the General to consult with them before resigning if, as seems to be the case, his resignation on January 20 was only to be the prelude to a later return to the midst of more tractable parties.

Whatever the reason, the Moderates and the Radicals who had participated on a personal basis in the De Gaulle government refused to participate in the cabinet formed by Félix Gouin. Tripartism in the exact sense of the word, having been prepared by the governments of national unanimity formed for the war and made possible by the triumph of the three big parties over the Moderates and the Radicals at the elections of October 21, 1945, was born on January 26, 1946 with the formation of the Gouin government.

It was apparent from the start that harmony among the three major parties was far from complete. If they were able to avoid serious conflict on the governmental level, such was not the case with respect to the constitutional problem, and the drafting of a constitution was the primary task of the Assembly. The Communists and the Socialists—the former by design, the latter out of fidelity to the old doctrine of their party rather than out of true conviction—drafted a plan of government by assembly without any of the counterbalancing elements, the checks on or divisions of power which provide in a democratic system the best guarantees against the dictatorship of a transient majority. The Popular Republicans were disposed toward establishing a system considerably more democratic than that of the constitution of 1875. During the Third Republic, the Senate held the same powers as the Chamber of Deputies, and its method of election, which gave greater representation to the rural areas, made it a permanent stronghold of conservatism. But the Popular Republicans also understood that the constitutional draft prepared by their partners might lead the way to the establishment in France of a "people's democracy" like those which were starting to operate in the countries occupied by the USSR, in eastern and central Europe, that is, to make possible the complete triumph of the Communists. Having entered the government after General de Gaulle's departure precisely for the purpose of avoiding such an eventuality, they had to oppose the constitution that the Socialists and the Communists wanted to impose on them. After many attempts at compromise, their leader, François de Menthon, resigned his position as *rapporteur* of the constitutional draft and, on April 19, they voted against the text prepared by the Socialist-Communist majority, which was adopted by 309 votes to 249.

The constitution voted by the Assembly could go into effect only if it were ratified by the voters at a referendum which was set for May 5. During the referendum campaign the propaganda of the parties demonstrated how basically superficial the political formula of tripartism actually was. The Communists supported the affirmative position with an extraordinary abundance of material means and an unusual profusion of arguments. The Socialists imitated them, but more discreetly, so much so that it appeared to the public as though the ratification of the constitution would be essentially a Communist victory. The MRP waged against the constitution, which had been drafted by its partners in the governmental coalition, a campaign comparable in intensity to that waged for the opposite side by the Communists. The Radicals and Moderates pooled their efforts, but as they did not have so efficient an organization as the Popular Republicans their propaganda seemed to follow rather than lead that of the MRP. General de Gaulle, who many voters hoped would advise them how to vote, did not break the silence which he had guarded since his resignation.

On May 5, the constitutional draft which had been approved in the Assembly with a majority of sixty votes was rejected by the country by a margin of more than a million votes: approved by 9,454,000 voters, it was rejected by 10,585,000. Because of the propaganda campaign which had preceded the referendum, the verdict of the voters represented a serious defeat for the Communist party. In fact, it is May 5, 1946, that marks the beginning of the decline of the influence exercised by the Communist party on French political life. Until this time, many people believed the legend of the inevitable progress of communism, in part as a delayed reaction to Vichy's propaganda. This had contributed to discourage many adversaries of the Communist party and had attracted to it people who wanted to be on the side of the strongest contestant. This legend was now unquestionably destroyed. It had been demonstrated that the party could be beaten and that it was not infallible. In fact, without minimizing the role of the propaganda of the advocates of a negative vote, it seems that the Communist party made a serious psychological error by waging too vigorous a campaign in favor of the constitution. The constitution might perhaps have been ratified if the Socialists had appeared to be its strongest advocates. It is likely that a large number of negative votes were motivated by the desire of Left or even extreme Left voters not to permit the Communists to represent the results of the referendum as their personal victory.

Although tripartism had been seriously damaged by the vote of May 5, it lasted through the election of the Second Constituent Assembly, which took place on June 2. There were noticeable changes in strength of the parties, however: the MRP, which appeared to be the great victor of the referendum, this time arrived at the head of the others. The Communists also gained a little. The Socialists suffered a serious decline. The Moderates and the Radicals (the latter now allied in the framework of the Rassemblement des Gauches Républicaines [RGR, Rally of the Republican Left] with the little group, l Union Démocratique et Socialiste de la Résistance [UDSR, Democratic-Socialist Union of the Resistance] composed of men who entered political life after the Liberation, many of whom were personally attached to General de Gaulle) gained only a little strength, as the MRP, enjoying the prestige it had acquired on May 5, continued to attract most of the votes of their former electorate. While the deputies for metropolitan France were divided equally between Marxists (146 Communists and 115 Socialists, making a total of 261) and non-Marxists (160 MRP, 39 RGR, and 62 Moderates, making a total also of 261), the voting in the overseas districts, in Algeria especially, returned a relatively large number of native nationalists disposed toward allying themselves with the Communists. This threw the balance in favor of the parties which had been beaten in the referendum of May 5. The majority of the new assembly was the same as that of the earlier one, although it was somewhat reduced in size.

The MRP did not want under any circumstances to become separated from the Socialists by entering a conservative coalition with the RGR and the Moderates. It believed that it was indispensable to change radically both the political institutions and the economic and social structure inherited from the Third Republic, and it could not get along with the advocates of a return to the *status quo ante bellum*. The Socialists, although their propaganda between May 5 and June 2 had taken on a sharp anti-Communist tone, were not in any way disposed to break with the Communist party. It was necessary to continue with tripartism. This is what was done on the governmental level under Georges Bidault, the leader of the MRP, and this is what the parties undertook to do on the constitutional level by making just enough changes in the constitutional draft rejected on May 5 to satisfy the MRP.

The position of the MRP, however, was made difficult by General de Gaulle. On June 16, after the first meeting of the Assembly but before the election of Georges Bidault as Premier, the Gen-

eral delivered a speech at Bayeux in which, after having lauded
the result of the referendum of May 5, he sketched the outlines
of a constitution which would create a system somewhat between
the presidential and parliamentary systems. He said that this was
the only system suitable for France in "the very difficult and very
dangerous era" which confronted her.[2] The role prescribed in this
speech for the President of the Republic—"to harmonize the general interest . . . with the orientation of Parliament . . . to serve
as arbiter of unexpected political difficulties . . . to exercise that
influence of continuity which a nation cannot do without . . .
if the country should be in danger, to be the guarantor of national
independence and of the treaties concluded by France"—indicated clearly that the General considered himself as called upon
to fill this exalted office. That is undoubtedly why, having learned
from experience of the difficulties he would have in coming to
terms with the parties represented in Parliament, he categorically
stated that "it went without saying that the executive power should
not emanate from Parliament."

Could the MRP adopt the constitutional program defined by
General de Gaulle and re-establish the contact with him that had
been broken on January 20? Nothing was more unlikely. A constitution like that described at Bayeux could not fail to evoke in
French opinion, always sensitive to historical references, the con-
sular system and the name of Bonaparte. The MRP wanted to
convince the traditional Left that Catholics could be as sincerely
republican and profoundly democratic as the Left was. To defend
a system which would inevitably be called Bonapartist would
mean failing in this task; it would mean condemning the MRP
to an alliance with the Right; it would mean assuming a hopeless
position, for it was certain that an assembly where the Communists and the Socialists constituted a majority, thanks to the
support of the Algerian, Madagascan, and African nationalists,
would never accept the constitution of Bayeux. Was it not essential that, two years after the Liberation, France have a permanent

[2] *L'Année Politique 1946*, pp. 534 ff.

set of institutions? Could it stand the risk of another negative referendum, of the election of a third provisional assembly? The General's program, moreover, hardly squared with the constitutional ideas of the Christian Democrats, who were inspired by the Catholic conception of society and not disposed toward the foundation of a powerful state capable of imposing its sovereign will on the various indigenous groups which emerge in the nation.

The Popular Republicans were obliged to seek a solution through a compromise with their partners in tripartism, since no positive solution could come from collaboration either with De Gaulle or with the Radical and Moderate opposition. But the electoral support of the MRP was Gaullist in sentiment and, because of its conservative tendencies, inclined to look favorably on the idea of a presidential system, of a strong state capable of imposing its authority on the babblers in Parliament. Would not the General's return to the political scene inevitably attract these voters and menace the MRP's position as the "first party of France?" The risk was a real one. The MRP resolved to run it, however, rather than to lose contact with the Socialists and allow themselves to be pushed toward the Right, thereby restoring the old division of the nation into two blocs of almost equal strength.

The Popular Republicans had no illusions about the cohesiveness and the durability of tripartism. They had resigned themselves to it in January only in order to prevent the Communists from moving unhindered down the road to a total conquest of power. The referendum of May 5 had been a reverse of the most decisive importance for the Communists. But the Communist party had learned from this failure and was going to change its methods.

Since the end of 1944, when it had allowed the "patriotic militia," which it largely controlled, to be disarmed and had let De Gaulle re-establish the authority of the state over the local Committees of Liberation, in which it played a major role, the Communist party appeared to have given up revolutionary methods and working-class agitation in order to concentrate its efforts on electoral propaganda and the legal conquest of a legislative mandate. In the social sphere especially, it had supported governmental policy; it had urged the working class to work and to maintain discipline, and it had accepted the freezing of wages at the level they had reached after the increases granted immediately after the Liberation. Its defeat of May 5, confirmed on June 2 by the lead which the MRP took over it, caused it to change its tactics. Right after the elections, even before the formation of the new government, the General Confederation of Labor, which the Communists dominated, demanded an increase in wages in order to compensate for the increase in prices and to alleviate for the workers the hardships created by the food shortages. It supported this demand with the threat of a general strike. The Communist party supported this demand on the political level, and the Popular Republicans and Socialists, in spite of their fear of setting off a new inflationary cycle, were forced to acquiesce. Through the menace of a general strike the Communist party partially re-established the prestige it had lost in the referendum of May 5.

The Socialist party also felt some aversion for the tripartite formula. It attributed its losses in the elections of June 2 to the concessions it had had to make, to its governmental connections with the MRP, which had separated it from the voters faithful to the class struggle, and to its constitutional agreement with the Communist party, which had caused it to lose the votes of those people who wanted above all to preserve liberty and to defend democracy. At the Lyons congress, in August 1946, Daniel Mayer, the secretary general of the party, a friend of Léon Blum and an advocate of relaxing the old formulas of Marxist orthodoxy in favor of a humanistic socialism quite close to certain conceptions of the MRP, was put in the minority and replaced by a strict Guesdist, Guy Mollet. But the congress stated at the same time [3] that the organic unity of the proletariat—that is, an alliance and

[3] *L'Année Politique 1946*, p. 209.

eventually fusion with the Communist party—was made impossible by "the political and intellectual subjugation" of the Communist party to the Russian state and by the fact that it did not practice "genuine working-class democracy." The Lyons congress put an end to the Socialist-Communist co-ordinating committee which had been formed on December 4, 1944. It expressed the hope that circumstances might permit the formation of an exclusively Socialist government.

In spite of all these fissures, tripartism continued to survive. The Bidault government remained in power throughout the duration of the Assembly which had been elected on June 2. After laborious negotiations, the first constitutional draft was doctored with some amendments that were more apparent than real. A second chamber, the Council of the Republic, was created and endowed with a minimum of power, and a more important role was given the President of the Republic. This permitted the MRP to say that it was satisfied for the moment, while it reserved the right later to propose a revision of the text for which it had voted. On the morning of September 30 the draft was approved by 440 votes to 106, with only the Moderates and most of the members of the RGR refusing to accept it. The very day that the Assembly voted, General de Gaulle made a speech at Epinal condemning the constitutional draft adopted by the tripartite majority and urging the voters to reject it. Communists, Socialists, and Popular Republicans, on the other hand, campaigned, more discreetly than they had in May, in favor of the constitution. But one of the principal arguments of the Popular Republicans was that the constitution was "perfectible," and they tried to demonstrate that their favorable attitude, combined with their desire for future revision, hardly differed basically from the plainly hostile attitude of General de Gaulle. The only difference between them, they implied, was in their estimation of the difficulties that would be created by the election of a new constituent assembly for a period of seven months. The constitution was ratified on October 13, but only because there were many abstentions. It received 9,297,000 affirmative votes, that is, fewer than the first draft received; but there were only 8,165,000 negative votes, the number of abstentions having increased from 5,262,000 to 8,520,000. It was obvious that a large proportion of the MRP's voters, and undoubtedly even some of the Socialists', had preferred to abstain, torn as they were between the counsels of their party and those of General de Gaulle. Perhaps the increase in the number of abstentions was due also to the fact that the political significance of the vote was not as clear as it had been in May, as the prestige of no party was as closely tied as it had been then to the acceptance or the rejection of the constitutional draft.

The National Assembly was to be elected—for five years—four weeks after the referendum. An electoral campaign started which struck new blows at the cohesion of tripartism. The MRP, for which the reconquest of the voters who had not followed its advice on October 13 was of major importance, launched the slogan "Bidault without Thorez," published leaflets contrasting "voting Communist" and "voting French," and let it be understood very clearly that it was resolved to force the Communist party into the opposition. The Socialists, in conformity with the decisions of their congress, emphasized their independence from both the MRP and the Communist party. Although the Moderate and Radical opposition, allied in quite a few departments with a group called the Gaullist Union (from which the General, however, remained completely apart), based its entire campaign on a criticism of tripartism, none of the participants in the tripartite government actually defended it; each of them attacked indiscriminately its partners in the old majority.

On November 10 the Communist party became the largest party once again by picking up some 300,000 votes; the MRP lost 500,000 votes; the Socialist party lost 600,000 votes; the Radical, Gaullist, and Moderate opposition gained more than 300,000 votes; the number of abstentions was much larger than it had been in June. It looked as though the Popular Republicans had succeeded in winning back most of the voters who had deserted them on October 13. It is likely that this would not have been the case if General de Gaulle had personally supported the candidates of the opposition. But his aloofness from the Gaullist Union had given the impression that he did not want to mix in partisan struggles and again allowed the MRP to obtain the votes of many people who were basically supporters of De Gaulle.

The decline of the Socialists and of the Algerian Nationalists created a major change in the composition of the Assembly relative to that of the two Constituent Assemblies. This time the Marxist parties and their satellites from overseas no longer enjoyed an absolute majority; they could muster only 296 votes out of 618.

The widening of the breaches in the tripartite bloc provoked by the electoral campaign was demonstrated strikingly in December when the National Assembly had to elect the president of the provisional government (Premier), who was to remain in office until the election of the Council of the Republic and the naming of the President of the Republic by the members of the two parliamentary assemblies made it possible to put the new constitution in operation. The Communist party, under the pretext that it was the largest party in the Assembly, demanded the premiership and presented its secretary general, Maurice Thorez, as its candidate. The Socialists, certain that Thorez had no chance of winning enough votes to be elected, decided to vote for him in order to satisfy, without running any serious risks, those militants who still believed in the principle of working-class unity and, especially, in order to obtain in return Communist support for the Socialist candidate for the post of President of the Republic. Twenty-five Socialist deputies, however, refused to vote for the Communist leader, who received only 259 votes, while he needed 310 to be elected. The MRP then presented Georges Bidault as a candidate, but he received only 240 votes, as the Socialists, the Radicals, and some of the Moderates refused to vote for him. In order to end the deadlock, the Socialists proposed Léon Blum as a candidate. Blum's personal prestige was great enough to compensate for the fact that his party was only the third largest in the Assembly and that it had lost many votes on November 10. Blum was elected on December 12 by 575 votes.

It became apparent when Blum tried to form his ministry that his election by almost the entire Assembly signified in no way the resurrection of tripartism. The Communists demanded that one of the three portfolios of the Interior, Foreign Affairs, or National Defense be given to one of their representatives, and the MRP absolutely refused to accede to this demand. On the other hand, Léon Blum wanted to ask for the collaboration of the Moderates and the RGR, but the Communists refused to go any farther to the Right than the Radical group. It was because of these circumstances that the desires of the Socialist militants could be temporarily satisfied. Léon Blum formed an exclusively Socialist ministry, counting on the support of the other groups to last until mid-January, when the President of the Republic would be elected. In order to end the deadlock, the Popular Republicans, Communists, and Radicals accepted this solution, but only because it was not to last longer than a month. The fate of tripartism was obviously in jeopardy. The Communist party had decided to restore tripartism only if it could secure more influence in the future government than it had had in earlier ones. The MRP was resolved to reduce the influence of the Communists in the government. The Socialists, basically of the same opinion as the MRP, were thinking for the moment mainly about not spoiling the chances of their future candidate for the Presidency of the Republic by antagonizing one of the parties whose votes would be necessary for his election.

The Radical and Moderate minority, faced with the prospects of a rupture of the tripartite majority formed at the beginning of 1946, were divided as to what tactic to follow. For some, the Moderates of the Republican Party of Liberty and the Radicals influenced by Edouard Daladier, it was necessary to maintain a position of inflexible opposition to the parties which were wholly or partly responsible for the direction of public affairs since the

Liberation. Their plan was to let the future bring them their revenge and restore to the present minority all the levers of command; and they wanted no compromise with their opponents.

For others, the Moderates of the Independent Republican group
and the Radicals faithful to Edouard Herriot, it was necessary to
avoid any sort of intransigence, to accept if necessary collaboration
in office with the three major parties. Their plan was to create,
little by little, a new balance of power which would enable the
minority gradually to extend its influence over public affairs.

Some of the opponents of tripartism were therefore ready to
collaborate with it in the hope of hastening its collapse. This situation was quite different from that established in January 1946,
and it contained an additional threat to the already-fragile governmental formula which had been inaugurated at that time. Not
only did the parties which had supported tripartism hesitate to
continue it, but some of its earlier opponents were now willing
to make tactical concessions for the purpose of hastening its down-
fall. In spite of appearances, during the first weeks which followed the convocation of the National Assembly there were many
reasons for thinking that there would be a shift in the balance of
power which had existed since the resignation of General de
Gaulle.

The End of Tripartism: January–October 1947

Parliament, consisting of the members of the National Assembly and the Council of the Republic, met at Versailles on
January 16, 1947, to elect the President of the Republic. The
schisms of tripartism, complicated by personal ambitions, again
became evident when the candidates were presented. The Socialist party presented Vincent Auriol, the president of the National Assembly, and the MRP opposed him with Champetier de
Ribes, the president of the Council of the Republic. The Radical
opposition supported the dean of the Council of the Republic,
M. Gasser, and the Moderates supported the President of the PRL
[Republican Party of Liberty], Michel Clemenceau. The Com-

munist party let it be understood several hours before the balloting that it would vote for Vincent Auriol. The Communists and
the Socialists alone did not have the absolute majority of the
members of Parliament necessary to elect the President; it was
therefore possible that it would be necessary to hold a second
ballot, which would have given some useful indications of the
possibilities of agreement among the parties. But Auriol was
elected on the first ballot, receiving 452 votes out of 883 cast. In
addition to the Socialists and the Communists, about forty members of the other parties had voted for him. It seems that this support came especially from the Radicals of the Herriot group. The
election of the President of the Republic demonstrated once again
how fragile the tripartite political formula had become.

Tripartism appeared, however, to take on new strength when,
after Léon Blum's resignation, a cabinet was formed by Paul
Ramadier, one of the most moderate leaders of the Socialist party,
whom Auriol had named as Premier and who had won the confidence of the Communist party and of the MRP. After certain
difficulties arising out of the Communists' demands concerning
the distribution of portfolios, he finally succeeded in securing from
these two parties the co-operation that Léon Blum had not been
able to get in December. This time, however, tripartism was
greatly extended, for five members of the RGR and two Moderates
also entered the new cabinet. This cabinet appeared to be a transition between the old tripartism and a new political formula in
which the influence of the Marxist Left would be diminished and
in which Communist influence would undoubtedly soon be completely eliminated. But the latter step required an auspicious moment. If the MRP agreed in January 1947 to collaborate with the
Communists, something that it had refused to do in December, it
was only because it seemed wiser to wait a few weeks longer before
taking concrete measures to remove them from positions of power.

There were two problems over which the parties of the majority
were shortly to become divided: economic policy and policy in
Indo-China. Léon Blum's cabinet had tried to lower prices by

government action, which required freezing of wages; and Ramadier had announced in his ministerial declaration his desire to
continue this policy. On this point, only the Communists differed from the other parties in the government. The Communists
claimed, somewhat paradoxically, that the decrease in prices could
and must be accompanied by an increase in wages. The food
shortages, which were still very severe at this time, caused unrest
which was manifested by strikes in many areas. These strikes
furnished the CGT unions, which were controlled by the Communists, with an opportunity to stir up agitation that placed
great difficulties in the way of the success of the government's
economic policy.

Since December 19, 1946, hostilities had broken out again in
Indo-China between the Viet Minh nationalist party, which was
largely infiltrated by Communists and which was led by Ho Chi
Minh, and French troops. The Communists recommended opening negotiations with Ho Chi Minh and declared that it was the
French High Commissioner, Admiral Thierry d'Argenlieu, who
bore the real responsibility for the Viet Minh offensive of December 19 because of his provocations. The Moderates, Radicals, and
Popular Republicans thought, on the other hand, that Ho Chi
Minh had never had any sincere intention of coming to an understanding with the French. They felt that his real aim was to break
all relations between Indo-China and the French Union and that,
rather than to undertake negotiations that were doomed to fail,
it was necessary to subdue with force the Communist insurrection
that he led. The Socialists were divided on the question. Some of
them, especially the Minister for Overseas France, Marius Moutet,
were opposed to reopening negotiations. But the pacifist and anti-
colonialist tradition of the party tended to make the opinion of
many of its members identical with that of the Communists: they
were opposed to the extension of military operations and wanted
to reopen negotiations.

The concrete issue which was being presented when the majority eventually collapsed was a factor of great importance.

The political consequences of a breach over the question of Indo-China would have been quite different from those following a breach over economic policy. The Communists were isolated on the economic issue, while the Socialist party would remain more or less allied with the Communists on the Indo-Chinese question, and there might be no new majority in the National Assembly except an alliance of the MRP with the RGR and the entire Right.

It was the Indo-Chinese problem which arose first. On March 5 a Radical member of the Council of the Republic, M. Bollaert, was named High Commissioner to replace Admiral d'Argenlieu. The latter's departure satisfied the Socialists, and his successor reassured the MRP and the Radicals. A great debate over Indo-China took place in the National Assembly between March 11 and 18. Party solidarity required the Socialists, even those who did not share the opinions of the Minister for Overseas France and the Premier, to approve their policy. This policy was defined as "resistance to violence and the desire for peace and harmony," but it contained this warning: "there are men with whom it will be impossible to deal." [4] This formula indicated clearly that there was no intention of opening negotiations with Ho Chi Minh.

The Communist party, however, did not let its disagreement with the rest of the majority lead it to break away completely. The Communist ministers voted for the order of the day approving the government's position, and the rest of the Communist group did not vote against the government, but abstained. The same procedure was followed several days later when the government made a question of confidence out of its request for military appropriations for its expeditionary corps. After some hesitation, Premier Ramadier decided to remain in office in spite of this desertion by part of his majority, for the affirmative vote of the Communist ministers had maintained the fiction of governmental solidarity.

The economic and social problem arose toward the end of April after a strike had broken out at the automobile plants of

4 See L'Année Politique 1947, p. 40.

the Régie Nationale Renault in support of a demand for a wage increase. The CGT did not start this strike, and it even, at first, tried to stop it. But the Communist party recognized that this was a genuine and spontaneous movement of the workers, and it did not want to oppose the proletarian masses in any way. The Communists brusquely changed their attitude and approved the strike, taking up the demand for a general increase in wages.

The conflict between the Communist ministers and the rest of the government was carried before the Assembly by Ramadier, who posed a question of confidence on a motion approving the continuation of the policy of price decreases and wage-freezing. On May 4 this motion was voted by 346 votes, but the 186 Communist deputies, including the ministers, voted against it. The next day Ramadier issued a decree terminating the functions of the members of the government who had voted against it on a motion of confidence. During the afternoon of the same day, the last Communist minister, M. Marrane, who, as he was a member of the Council of the Republic, had not had to take part in the vote of confidence and who had therefore not been discharged at the same time as his colleagues, handed in his resignation. Tripartism had ended.

Why were the Communists so intransigent in May when they had, in March, authorized their ministers to vote with the government on the question of Indo-China in order to prevent a rupture in the cabinet? It is certain that their decision can be partly explained by their appreciation of the discontent of the workers that was revealed by the strike at the Renault factories. As it relies especially on the proletariat for support, the Communist party would have been running a serious risk by directly opposing the wage claims which were really only the logical sequence of the demands that it had itself provoked and supported the preceding June. The fact that the Communist unions had not been able to prevent this strike was a warning that it could not ignore; but it could have found a compromise and did not have to destroy so abruptly the solidarity of the government.

The real explanation of its attitude must be sought in the area of foreign policy. The Moscow Conference had taken place in April 1947, and it had revealed the widening gap between the Soviet Union and the Anglo-Saxon powers. Until this time, Georges Bidault, the Minister of Foreign Affairs, had tried to maintain a balance between France's allies of the East and of the West. But at the Moscow Conference the Soviet Union refused to accede to French claims with respect to German coal and the disposition of the Saar. France was forced to choose, and she aligned herself with the Western powers.

It is clear that the French Communists' conciliatory attitude in March over the Indo-China question was due to their desire to remain in the government as long as that would enable them to influence French foreign policy in a direction favorable to the Soviet point of view. But at the end of April, at the time of the crisis caused by the Renault strike, the Moscow Conference had ended with a break between the USSR and France and with an unquestionable *rapprochement* between France and the Anglo-Saxon powers. As the participation of the Communists in the government had not produced the diplomatic consequences which they regarded as of major importance, they no longer had the same reasons that they had had six weeks earlier for preserving at least the appearance of ministerial solidarity. This is the basic reason for the hostile votes cast on May 4 by the Communist ministers against the government in which they were participating, votes which could only lead to their removal from office.

At the very moment when the balance of political forces that had existed for sixteen months was overthrown by the intransigence of the Communists and the refusal of their partners to give in any longer to the blackmail that the Communists had been extorting since June 1946 through the threat of strikes, General de Gaulle returned to French political life. His return was to have as important consequences as the departure of the Communists from the government.

During a patriotic ceremony held on March 30 in the town of

Bruneval in Normandy, De Gaulle delivered a speech that was mainly devoted to praising the operational intelligence organizations of the Resistance but the last passages of which were of a political nature. "The day will come," he said, "when setting aside its sterile quarrels and reforming a badly constructed framework which misguides the nation and cripples the state, the great mass of Frenchmen will rally to France." At Strasbourg a week later, on April 7, the General made another speech, this time devoted entirely to the political situation. After criticizing the activity of the parties and the constitution, he sketched a governmental program and concluded by saying that "it is time that we form . . . the *Rassemblement du Peuple Français* [Rally of the French People] which, within the framework of the laws, will promote and assure the triumph, above differences of opinions, of a great movement for the general welfare and the profound reform of the state." [5] Finally, on April 14, in a statement to the press, the General announced that he was going to create an organization, the Rassemblement du Peuple Français (RPF), which he invited all Frenchmen to join regardless of the parties to which they belonged. The major objective of the RPF would be to revise the constitution in order to liberate the state from the control of the parties.

The General did not conceive of the RPF as a political party in the exact sense of the word. His intention was to go beyond the existing parties and to create an organization which would give a common direction to their activities for the purpose of achieving certain objectives essential for the public welfare. De Gaulle certainly wanted to find members for his Rassemblement in every area of political opinion and not to link it in any way with any special group.

All the parties, however, did not react in the same way to De Gaulle's venture. Since the Bruneval speech, the Communists had accused De Gaulle of having become "the leader of reaction"; after the Strasbourg speech, the Socialist party declared that "with-

[5] See the complete text of the speech in *L'Année Politique 1947*, pp. 323–326.

out parties democracy cannot live" and decried the implication of personal power contained in the appeal for a rallying of political forces around the General. The Socialist party told its militants to be vigilant in the defense of democratic institutions. A little later, on April 27, the national committee of the MRP decided that the Popular Republicans would not be authorized to join the RPF.

These reactions were predictable, and they were all the more inevitable as, since they were preparing to break with the Communists and thus be treated as "enemies of the Left," neither the Socialists nor the Popular Republicans could run the risk of being criticized for supporting one of those attempts to establish personal rule which have always been considered in France as the most serious danger which can be raised against the Republic. The formation of the RPF, its revisionist aims, its hostility toward the parties, its desire to reinforce the state by establishing presidential power—all that necessarily evoked in the minds of democrats the antiparliamentary leagues of the time of Boulanger and of the Dreyfus Affair, without mentioning those that had arisen in France during the last years of the Third Republic.

In order to forestall an unfavorable attitude on the part of the Socialist party, De Gaulle would have had to make preliminary contacts with its leaders, to be extremely diplomatic, to give them convincing guarantees of the sincerity of his democratic intentions, but it is still not certain that even this attitude would have been enough to remove the distrust of most of the Socialist militants. But the General's temperament had not permitted him to take such precautions, and the way in which he announced the creation of the RPF really left him no hope of securing even the neutrality of the Socialist party.

The unfavorable reaction of the MRP was not quite so inevitable. The party which had claimed in 1945 to be the "party of fidelity" had many men who were personally attached to De Gaulle among its leaders, and the referendum of October 13, 1946, had proved that a very large number of its voters shared these

sentiments. But the fundamental purpose of the Christian Democrats who had formed the MRP had been to destroy the traditional
identification of the French Catholics with the conservative and
reactionary Right by creating new links with the parties of the
Left, whose program for social emancipation, political liberty,
and human progress was to a great extent inspired by the Christian tradition of Western civilization. In many respects, therefore,
friendship with the Socialist party was a fundamental necessity for
the MRP. By allowing its militants and its members of Parliament to enter the orbit of the RPF it would have inevitably ended
this friendship. This the MRP could not do, all the more as
those MRP leaders who had been ministers under General de
Gaulle doubted that his temperament would enable him to become in peacetime the head of a democratic, parliamentary state.

From the start, the negative attitude adopted by the Socialists
and then by the Popular Republicans toward the RPF condemned
the latter to take on a character quite different from the one which
its founder wanted to give it. Neither the Moderate parties (the
PRL and the Peasant party) nor the RGR were unfavorable to the
RPF. On the contrary, they tolerated the "double membership"
of their militants and their members of Parliament in the RPF
and in their own organizations. The RPF was therefore composed
exclusively either of nonpartisans, many of whom were conservative, or of members of the parties of the Right or of the Center
Right. That gave it from the start not the character of a true rally
of the French but of a regrouping of the conservatives forces. This
new group would inevitably come into conflict with those who
claimed to represent, as the Socialists always had or as the Popular
Republicans had for a shorter period, the essential elements of the
republican tradition and of the *mystique* of the Left. But whatever the future of the RPF was to be, it was certain that at the very
moment when the break with the Communists was going to make
it necessary to extend the parliamentary majority toward the
Center and even toward the Right Center, a powerful source of attraction was going to separate from this eventual majority not only

many of the Moderates and Radicals, whose support would be necessary, but perhaps even some of the members of its largest constituent element, the MRP.

The attraction of the RPF for the Right and the Right Center had not yet become evident on May 4. Although Ramadier had expressly invited the advocates of a presidential system, which meant the Gaullists, to vote against the government, only the Communists had voted against it, part of the conservatives and some members of the RGR being content with abstaining. At this time the Right wanted in no way to weaken the position of a government which had decided to break with the Communists and force them into the opposition. In addition, in spite of the encouraging growth of the RPF's membership, the RPF was still too recent a creation and the importance it was going to have in French political life could not be fully grasped.

Once the Communist ministers were ejected, however, the question arose of whether the Socialist party would, contrary to the attitude it had constantly held since November 1945, agree to remain in power in co-operation only with parties on its right. The national council of the Socialist party was convoked to decide this question. The circumstances surrounding the break were favorable for Ramadier's position; he wanted to be authorized by his party to remain in power. If the break had taken place over the question of Indo-China, the majority of the Socialist militants would have undoubtedly demanded the resignation of the cabinet. But the program of decreasing prices which had been started by the Socialist government of Léon Blum in January, and which had awakened great hope in the country, appeared to the Socialists to be their own exclusive contribution to the coalition government's program. It still bore the stamp of Léon Blum's prestige. To leave power because the Communist party had opposed this policy would have meant that the Socialist party was renouncing its own originality and sacrificing its very autonomy. On the other hand, the creation of the RPF permitted it, at the same time that it broke with the Communists, to take up a position of hostility toward a new, menacing Right and therefore not to appear to be collaborating with enemies of the Republic. These considerations, which modified the opinion of a number of militants, were enough to reverse the majority opinion of the preceding Socialist party congress. On May 7, by 2,529 votes to 2,125, the national council of the Socialist party pronounced itself in favor of the continuance of the Ramadier government despite the passage of the Communists into the opposition.

The political situation had greatly changed. The Socialists and Popular Republicans did not together have a majority in the National Assembly, and the support of a certain number of votes from the RGR and the Moderates was indispensable to the survival of the cabinet. The liberals, who had seemed to be hostages of the Socialists and of the socialistically inclined members of the MRP when they joined the majority in January, found their tactical situation completely transformed. The government now depended on their support and they would be able to demand important concessions, both of an economic and a political nature, in return. It was not long before the RGR's offensive started against the *dirigisme* of the Socialist Minister of National Economy, André Philip. On more than one occasion, especially when the financial bills were voted in June, the RGR put the cabinet in danger. But the attack was never pushed to its logical extreme; the Radicals and the Moderates did not want to risk a governmental crisis which might lead the Socialists to refuse to return to power without the participation of the Communists. They were content with making their gains by inches. However, a certain amount of tension developed between the militants of the Socialist party and its ministers when the voting of the electoral law for the municipal elections which were to take place in October and the statute for Algeria enabled the RGR and the Moderates to exact important concessions of a political nature from the Socialists.

The attraction of the RPF for the conservatives and the members of the RGR in the National Assembly was not long in becoming apparent. It is to this that the gradual reduction of Ramadier's majority must be attributed. This majority, 360 votes on May 4, fell to 331 on July 4 after an interpellation on the economic policy of the government and then fell to 292 on September 5 during the voting of a subsidy for the purpose of avoiding an increase in the price of coal. The RPF, after completing a preliminary exposition of its objectives by taking a position of categorical hostility to the Communist party, which De Gaulle called "separatist," [6] organized on August 20 an "intergroup" in the National Assembly. The majority of the Moderates, some members of the RGR, and even some Popular Republicans, who were later excluded from the MRP, joined this intergroup. The RPF now had an instrument for intervening directly in parliamentary activities. At the same time, the RPF announced that it would participate in the municipal elections by presenting everywhere lists of candidates "including men and women of diverse political beliefs." This decision gave the Moderates and the Radicals the opportunity to avenge the earlier electoral defeats of 1945 and 1946 by participating in a coalition which had every chance of success due to the prestige of General de Gaulle and the dissatisfaction of a large part of the population with the continuing economic difficulties, the shortages of food, and the rising prices.

Because of this situation the Radicals and the Moderates who had until then supported the Ramadier government were tempted to withdraw their support and to go into the opposition. The possibility of a new agreement between the Socialists and the Communists had become more and more unlikely due to the evolution of the international situation, especially because of the violent opposition of the Communists (obviously dictated by Soviet Russia) to the Marshall Plan and because of the reappearance of the Third International camouflaged as the Information Bureau of the Communist parties, or Cominform. This was one more reason for the liberals to deal less cautiously with the Socialists. But the doctrinaire militants of the Socialist party found it in-

[6] In a speech at Rennes on July 27; see *L'Année Politique 1947*, p. 326.

creasingly difficult to accept the compromises and the deals that Ramadier was forced to make with the right wing of his majority in order to remain in power. The political situation was therefore quite strained, and relations between the parties of the majority were extremely tenuous when the municipal elections were held on October 13 and 20, 1947.

In most of the large cities, including Paris, the RPF presented coalition lists with the Moderate parties and the RGR. It enjoyed a striking success, conquering the city halls of almost all the large cities and winning a large majority in the municipal council in Paris. In the countryside, where the balloting had a less pronounced political character and where the RPF had not yet had time to become organized, the Moderates and the Radicals gained substantially in many areas without the endorsement of General De Gaulle. The Communists lost votes, but their decline was limited; however, when the mayors were elected, coalitions were formed against them almost everywhere, and this deprived them of a considerable number of mayoralties which they had held since 1945. The Socialists maintained their position and even won some mayoralties thanks to the votes of the RPF councilors who preferred a Socialist mayor to a Communist one. The MRP suffered a veritable disaster. In the cities of more than 9,000 inhabitants, where the election took place under proportional representation, the MRP lost almost three-fourths of the votes it had won in 1946; in the small towns which it had not been able to penetrate because of its recent origin, its vote was unimpressive. It was clear that the great majority of the voters who had supported it in November 1946 had this time given their confidence to the Rassemblement of General de Gaulle. This upheaval of political forces in the country at once raised the question of whether the Ramadier government, which was supported by a majority of deputies who now represented only a minority of the electorate, could continue to exist. Tripartism was out of the question; a new political formula was needed.

The Attempt to Form a Third Force: November 1947

Those Socialists who had been dissatisfied with Ramadier's policy of compromising with the Moderates and the RGR saw the RPF as nothing but a reactionary organization that wanted to replace the Republic with a personal dictatorship. The RPF's victory in the municipal elections provoked these Socialists to take the initiative and formulate a policy for the purpose of defending the Republic simultaneously against the twin dangers which they thought were presented by the Communist party on the one hand and the Gaullist Rassemblement on the other. In addition, they wanted to formulate an economic and social policy that would protect the interests of the working classes and therefore deprive the two opposition groups of the advantages that they held because of the general dissatisfaction with high prices, reduced purchasing power, and food shortages.

The illusion of the possibility of complete Socialist independence, and hopes for an exclusively Socialist government had not survived the political developments of the first half of 1947. The necessity of close harmony between the Socialists and the Popular Republicans was accepted by the leaders of the Socialist party because the MRP's attitude toward the RPF had just proved that the Christian Democrats were firmly attached to the Republic and as aware as the Socialists were of the threat to the Republic that De Gaulle's aspirations to power might represent. In order to form a parliamentary majority, however, it was necessary to add to the Socialists and to the Popular Republicans a certain number of Radicals and even Moderates. It was hoped that opposition to the RPF's methods, attachment to the traditions of parliamentary government and, perhaps, also some hostility to De Gaulle personally, would be enough to persuade enough of the Radicals and Moderates to join a Center majority to defend the Republic and inaugurate a policy of reform.

This is the political formula which satisfied the frequently expressed desires of the founders of the MRP and to which its advocates—one of the most important of whom was Guy Mollet, the secretary general of the Socialist party—gave the name Third Force. The name was designed to indicate that the coalition intended to struggle against the two antagonistic forces, which were nevertheless frequently allied in the opposition, of Gaullism and communism. The two fundamental ideas of the promoters of the Third Force were that it should struggle equally against the dangers that both groups seemed to represent and that it would be able to endure only if it executed an active social policy and an effective economic policy. This meant, for them, refusing to make any concessions to liberalism and establishing a directed, if not a planned, economy. For a variety of reasons the realization of these goals required the removal of Ramadier as Premier. The present cabinet was becoming exhausted, and the Third Force proponents wanted to create a psychological shock by forming a new ministry.

Ramadier tried at first to stay in office. After the municipal elections he reorganized his government by reducing its size greatly and removing André Philip and Tanguy-Prigent, the Ministers of National Economy and of Agriculture. It was against these two men that most of the critics of *dirigisme* had directed their attacks. But the reorganized cabinet won a vote of confidence by only 300 votes to 280, thanks to the abstention of about twenty Moderates, followers of Paul Reynaud. About ten Popular Republicans had also abstained in order to emphasize their desire to have a new Premier, although their party had decided to continue to participate temporarily in the Ramadier government in order to avoid creating a crisis before the negotiations necessary for its solution were completed. It was obvious that the Ramadier cabinet was condemned, especially as the executive committee of the Socialist party decided to open negotiations immediately with the MRP and with "the Radicals who remained faithful to republican ideals" in order to form a "union of all true democrats." Ramadier himself then started to negotiate with the leaders of the different political groups, except the

Gaullists and the Communists, in order to make the way for his own successor. It was notable that he conversed with Paul Reynaud, thereby considerably enlarging the circle within which the leaders of his party had envisaged finding eventual partners for a new coalition. It seems that it was then believed on various sides that the excellent personal relations existing between Reynaud, the Moderate leader, and Léon Blum would enable the former to be included in a Third Force majority which would be assured of sizable strength on the Right because of his presence. It was very unlikely, however, that so convinced a liberal as Paul Reynaud could agree for very long with the Socialists on matters of economic policy.

The negotiations were moving along slowly when Guy Mollet, who undoubtedly wanted to hasten their conclusion, announced on November 19 in a speech before an Anglo-American press luncheon that the crisis, which theoretically had not even begun, would be settled within forty-eight hours, as Léon Blum was willing to become Premier. Ramadier certainly felt, and quite rightly, that Guy Mollet's optimism was premature and that Léon Blum was still not certain to get all the support he would need in order to form a "great Third Force ministry." But he was compelled to resign by the speech made by the secretary general of his own party, and he gave his resignation to the President that very evening.

The formation of a new government was especially urgent as unrest of a revolutionary nature was beginning to occur in various parts of the country, especially at Marseilles. The occasion for the unrest was the negotiation of a wage increase which had been accepted in principle by the Ramadier government in October, but over the size of which unions and the government were in disagreement. On November 20, Léon Blum was designated as Premier by the President. On November 21, he appeared before the National Assembly to solicit its confidence. His ministerial declaration [7] emphasized the basic ideas of the advocates of the

7 See *L'Année Politique 1947*, p. 330.

Third Force. "There is a double danger," he said, "On the one hand, international communism has openly declared war on French democracy. On the other hand, there has been formed in France a party whose goal—and perhaps whose only goal—is to deprive the national sovereignty of its fundamental rights." These remarks, which treated communism and Gaullism on the same level, irritated many Moderates and Radicals as well as some Popular Republicans. Many liberals undoubtedly also feared that the campaign against rising prices and for raising purchasing power to the highest level compatible with the capacity of the economy, as declared necessary by Léon Blum, could not be carried out without the continuance or the extension of economic controls, which they regarded as responsible for the slowness of economic recovery. Blum obtained only 300 votes in support of his program, while the constitution required 309 (an absolute majority of the members of the National Assembly, and not only of those voting) for the formation of a ministry. He was forced to give up his task.

According to Blum's own words, this vote indicated that what he had called the Third Force did not exist in the Assembly or, at least, that it was not "capable of becoming conscious of itself, of acting, and of governing." Two obstacles had prevented the "republican majority" from being formed: the refusal of its Moderate and Radical wing to oppose the Communist party and De Gaulle's RPF with the same vigor, and hesitation to give its indorsement to an economic policy inspired by Socialist principles. It would be necessary, as Léon Blum had himself said, to face the consequences of this fact, to try to form a majority which would undoubtedly be less cohesive both from the point of view of what it opposed as well as what it proposed, but which would be large enough to produce a government that could satisfy the numerical requirements of the constitution. Because of this, the Moderate Right and the Radical Center—all the liberals—were going to exert on future governments a leverage that was almost irresistible.

The Enlarged Third Force: November 1947–June 1951

The Third Force had not been able to find the support of an adequate majority in the National Assembly. The restoration of tripartism was out of the question. The Communists were carrying out a vast wave of insurrectionary strikes in the country, and their opposition to all the other parties over foreign policy had become more and more acute since the inauguration of the Marshall Plan. There was no way to resolve the political situation except to reconstitute the majority which had supported the Ramadier government since May or, if this failed, to dissolve the National Assembly and hold new elections. The latter solution was the one demanded by the RPF. General de Gaulle argued that the municipal elections of October had demonstrated that the strength of the different political groups was changed, and he demanded that the Assembly vote a new electoral law re-establishing a majority system and that it then end its own mandate. The latter could be done only by a law, as the conditions prescribed by the constitution for the dissolution of the Assembly by presidential decree had not been fulfilled. There was no majority in the Assembly, however, disposed towards satisfying the RPF's demands. The Socialist party and the MRP could not agree to give way to the RPF without first having tried to prove that the "regime of parties," now rid of the burden of the Communists, was capable of governing the country effectively. The Popular Republicans were deeply attached to proportional representation and had no desire to give it up. Many Radicals and Moderates, even those who had made or condoned alliances with the RPF at the municipal elections, considered the voting of a new electoral law impossible and new elections as hardly desirable in the atmosphere of agitation that had been created by the strikes. Moreover, the dissolution of the National Assembly as a result of the municipal elections would have seriously damaged the principle of representative government. The Assembly that was elected for five years at the end of 1946 retained the legal right to represent the country. A serious element of instability would have been introduced if the Assembly's mandate were to be ended after a municipal election which, except in the large cities, had not had as clearly a political character as the Gaullists claimed. Finally, the wave of strikes which was spreading from the south to all the industrial areas, especially in northern France, and which was accompanied by sabotage and violation of the freedom of labor, did not permit any hesitation. A government had to be formed rapidly so that the necessary steps could be taken to insure the operation of the public services. Public order had to be maintained in the face of the revolutionary character of the work stoppages. Encouragement had to be given to the many workers who, as the partisan nature of the movement in which the CGT was trying to lead them gradually became clearer, indicated their desire to go back to work as soon as it would be physically possible. This tense atmosphere explains in part the refusal of the majority of the Radical deputies and of a significant number of Moderates to support the RPF's position by preventing the formation of any government which would not surrender to the Gaullist ultimatum. The major reason, however, for their attitude in favor of compromising with the parties of the Third Force was that, although they had been quite willing to make use of the RPF for the municipal elections, they were not at all willing to allow themselves to be used by De Gaulle. This fact helps to reduce to its proper proportions the Gaullist victory in the municipal elections. Rather than being exclusively an RPF victory, it was the victory of a coalition that the leaders of the Rassemblement were far from able to control.

After Léon Blum's failure to win the confidence of the Assembly, President Auriol named Robert Schuman as Premier. Schuman had been the Minister of Finance in the preceding cabinet and, one of the leaders of the MRP, he was highly respected by the members of all the parties for his integrity. A deputy since 1919, Schuman had many friends on the Moderate benches of the Assembly, where he had himself sat at the beginning of his career, before he joined the Christian Democratic movement. He appeared before the National Assembly on the evening of November 22 and read a brief and simple statement,[8] the main characteristic of which was that it closed the door on no one who would support the government in its attempts to defend the Republic.

Schuman was invested by 412 votes, the only opposition being the 186 Communists and crypto-Communists. Some Gaullists had abstained, but almost all the Moderates and the Radicals had voted for him. Preoccupation with the strikes, the desire to erase the bad impression caused by Léon Blum's failure, and the satisfaction on the Right and in the Center with the abandonment of the idea of a struggle on two fronts, against the Gaullists as well as against the Communists, were the reasons for this overwhelming success. Schuman tried to get the simultaneous collaboration of Paul Reynaud in the Ministry of Economic Affairs and of Léon Blum for Social Affairs, but the contradiction between the liberal economic ideas of Paul Reynaud and those of the Socialists caused this plan to fail. It was finally a Radical, René Mayer, who took over the Finance Ministry, while his Socialist namesake, Daniel Mayer, continued to be Minister of Labor.

The ministry, which was formed during the night between Sunday, November 23, and Monday, November 24, presented itself before the National Assembly on November 27. The order of the day expressing confidence in the government, opposed by the 186 Communists, was carried by only 322 votes. Most of the Moderates and part of the RGR abstained, although they had voted for Schuman's investiture. The same phenomenon was to reoccur more than once in the course of the following years. The differences between parties, which become complicated by personal rivalries, always take on a more concrete and bitter character during the negotiations over the formation of a cabinet than they do during the more theoretical debate which precedes a vote on the investiture of a Premier.

[8] The complete text is in *L'Année Politique 1949*, p. 331.

In any event, in spite of the handicap of the RPF's success at the municipal elections and Léon Blum's failure, Robert Schuman had succeeded in re-forming the majority that had supported the Ramadier cabinet after the departure of the Communist ministers. In varying combinations this majority composed of Socialists, Popular Republicans, most of the RGR, and some Moderates was going to last until the spring of 1951, the date of the expiration of the National Assembly elected in November 1946. The majority was inherently unstable because of the differences of opinion among its constituent elements, especially with respect to economic and social affairs. After each crisis, however, it had to be formed again because the parties which composed it shared in common the desire to resist the revolutionary activity of the Communists without ceding all the levers of command to the RPF.

The details of the events which took place between the formation of the Schuman government and the spring of 1951 are unimportant for a study whose purpose is to analyze the basic political trends of the Fourth Republic. The general line of development between November 1947 and the spring of 1951 should, however, be traced briefly in order to present the complete background of the present situation.

The Schuman government succeeded in subduing the insurrectionary strikes of the fall of 1947 which led to a schism in the CGT. The anti-Communist elements withdrew in order to create a new central union, the CGT Force Ouvrière. The government enacted, not without difficulty, anti-inflationary measures in January 1948 (the Mayer withholding tax). But in the spring of 1948 it ran into difficulties in connection with the school problem. Certain mining companies which had been nationalized in 1946 owned Catholic schools. The question arose of what would become of them after the nationalization act went into effect. The Socialists, attached to the principle of secularism which had dominated the educational policy of the Third Republic, wanted them turned into public schools. The MRP, on the contrary, wanted them preserved as church schools wherever the parents of the pupils desired it. All attempts to compromise failed. Finally, the schools were secularized, thanks to the addition of Communist votes to those of the Socialists and of most of the Radicals. This was a bitter experience for the MRP. On the other hand, the Socialists reproached the MRP because one of its ministers, Mme. Poinso-Chapuis, had signed a decree permitting the departments and the towns indirectly to subsidize private schools through the intermediary of family associations. As a result of obstruction by the Socialist ministers, the administrative regulations necessary to put this decree into effect were never signed, and it remained a dead letter.

The disputes engendered by the question of the private schools strained relations between the Popular Republicans and the Socialists. The Schuman government suffered from the dissatisfaction concerning the agreement signed at London in the spring of 1948 on the subject of Germany. It also suffered from the exhaustion which very quickly strikes a government supported by a heterogeneous coalition and whose policy cannot satisfy any of its participants. The Socialists deserted it during a debate over military appropriations which they wanted reduced, and the government fell in July 1948.

The main consequence of this ministerial crisis was to increase the influence of the Radicals. They were given the premiership, which was confided to André Marie, who succeeded in getting the aid of both Léon Blum and Paul Reynaud. As could be expected, however, Reynaud's proposals for economic and financial matters aroused the opposition of the Socialists. As its members could not reach agreement, the government had to resign at the end of August, only one month after its formation.

Robert Schuman was again named and invested as Premier, but his cabinet could not find a majority to support it. Schuman had given the Ministry of Finance and Economic Affairs to a Socialist, Christian Pineau, and the liberals of the RGR and of the Moderate bloc, who usually supported the enlarged Third

Force, refused to give him their confidence. The ministry was reversed the very same day it presented itself to the National Assembly.

It had been proved that neither the liberals, with Paul Reynaud, nor the Socialists, with Christian Pineau, were able to make their views prevail fully. It is true, however, that the liberals were continually gaining ground by following a purely pragmatic policy of meeting difficulties one at a time, of refusing to apply any large-scale plan inspired by a pre-established doctrine, and even by occasionally making certain concessions to their opponents, concessions that were necessary from the point of view of parliamentary tactics but destructive of the coherence of the government's economic policy.[9] This is the method which had to be resorted to in September 1948 when the Queuille government was formed and in which financial policy was confided to a Moderate, Maurice Petsche.

In the fall, the government was faced with serious social problems which followed upon a long miners' strike encouraged by the Communist party. It succeeded in solving them. The political astuteness of the Premier—an astuteness which did not preclude frankness, since he was led to justify the sacrifices he demanded from each of the parties which supported him by stating brutally that they were "condemned to live together" because of the impossibility of forming any other majority—succeeded in making this government endure until the beginning of October 1949. Cantonal elections had been held in the spring and their results had seemed to prove that the country approved of the Center coalition. The RPF and the Communist party together won less than half the votes. But in the fall of 1949, the discontent of the Socialists exploded over a demand for a wage increase which was justified by the rise in the cost of living but which the Premier, supported

[9] For example, having restored a free market for gold, René Mayer, in January 1948, was forced, in order to maintain the support of the Socialists, to withdraw from circulation all 5,000-franc notes, which greatly reduced public confidence in the currency.

by Maurice Petsche, refused to accept out of fear of reopening the inflationary cycle. The government collapsed.

The ministerial crisis was long and difficult. Two successive Premiers who had been invested by the National Assembly, a Socialist, Jules Moch, and a Radical, René Mayer, had to give up trying to form a government, as they were unable to obtain the support of all the elements of the old majority which they proposed to form again. It was finally Georges Bidault, the president of the MRP, who was successful, partly because of the lassitude of the members of Parliament and because of the concern that was aroused by a crisis which seemed insoluble, but also because of Bidault's exceptional shrewdness.

The Bidault government enacted a law re-establishing collective bargaining over wages, although wages were not entirely uncontrolled, as a minimum guaranteed wage had to be fixed by the government. But before the new system went into operation a special bonus was to be granted to wage earners. Dissatisfied with the way in which this bonus was arranged (payment of it was to be spread over a period of several months), the Socialist ministers left the government at the beginning of February 1950. Georges Bidault remained in office until June, however. At this time he was reversed when the Socialists refused to support him after a debate over the method of calculating an increase in the salaries of civil servants.

A Queuille ministry was overthrown at the beginning of July 1950 on the same day it appeared before the National Assembly because the Socialists and a sizable number of Popular Republicans refused to support it. This cabinet contained no Socialists and Radicals and Moderates were prominent in its membership. Its political orientation was emphasized by the presence of Paul Reynaud. It was proved once again that there was no clear liberal majority in the National Assembly any more than there was a frankly Socialist one. The international tension caused by the outbreak of the Korean War, however, diminished the intransigence of the parties. René Pleven, leader of the UDSR, succeeded in forming a cabinet in which the Socialists agreed to participate and in support of which the old majority of Socialists, Popular Republicans, most of the RGR, and some Moderates was formed once again. For the first time in many months it was not disagreement over economic questions which provoked the fall of this ministry in the spring of 1951. Pleven had included in his program the passage of a new electoral law designed to facilitate the operation of the parliamentary system by reducing the representation of the Communist party and by creating a certain solidarity between the governmental parties by substituting, at least partially, the majority principle for proportional representation. It was the inability of the parties which had been supporting him to agree on the details of this new law (the Radicals demanded a system with two ballots, and the Popular Republicans refused to accept this) which led René Pleven to resign on February 25, 1951.

Henri Queuille then returned to power once again, at the head of a government similar to the one that he had led from September 1948 to October 1949, composed of representatives of all the groups of the majority. He succeeded in reducing the intransigence of his Radical friends, achieved the passage of a new electoral law (which will be dealt with later), and secured the National Assembly's agreement to a plan to advance the elections by five months, so that they would take place in June instead of November.

Almost all the ministerial crises that have just been summarized had been provoked by the intransigence of the Socialists, who wanted to stop the trend toward liberalism in French economic policy and to defend the interests of the wage earners by procuring for them, in the absence of lower prices, substantial increases in wages. But the Socialist party was never able to achieve its aims. On the contrary, each crisis was followed by a reinforcement of the influence of the liberals on the majority and on the government. The marginal position of the Radicals and the Moderates, who were indispensable for the formation of a majority in the National Assembly, gave them an irresistible bargaining position, especially as part of the MRP was aware of the liberal preferences of its electors. The failure of the initial conception of the Third Force was reflected in the economic and social sphere by the exact opposite of what its promoters would have wanted. Not only could no new economic and social reforms be carried out after November 1947, but the working masses were not able to improve their standard of living in proportion to the considerable increase in production. There was significant economic recovery, aided by the Marshall Plan, and increased quantities of consumers' goods enabled all the French, even those belonging to the humblest classes, to improve their material situation with respect to the poverty of the first postwar years. But this improvement was proportionally much greater for the wealthy and the privileged than for the great mass of the people. That is what the Socialists had wanted to prevent, but the political situation made them the prisoners of the Radicals and of the Moderates because they wanted neither to leave the way open for the Gaullists nor to come to terms with the Communists, and were thus left with no effective way of making their views prevail. It must be added that the economic recovery and the increase in production did not relieve the governments of their traditional financial difficulties. The short-comings of French fiscal policy constantly resulted in large budgetary deficits which, in turn, necessitated increased taxes which were often difficult to get through Parliament.

But it was not only in economic and social affairs that the Radicals and Moderates gained ground from 1947 to 1951 thanks to their indispensability to the majority. In 1948 it was necessary to fix a permanent electoral law for the Council of the Republic, as the second Constituent Assembly had adopted only a provisional one. The desire of the Socialists and of the MRP to weaken the Communists, who constantly tried to sabotage the work of the Council of the Republic as well as that of the National Assembly, led them to accept an electoral system modeled after the one used for the election of the old Senate and magnifying the political influence of the small rural communities where the parties of the

Right and of the Center are particularly strong. In spite of the few powers conferred on the Council of the Republic it was not without importance that this new electoral system made the RGR, after the Council's renewal in 1948, its most important political group. From that time on the majority in the Council, consisting of Moderates, Gaullists, and part of the RGR, systematically refused to vote any increase in taxes under the pretext that the budgetary deficit was due to the nationalization and social security acts passed after the Liberation. The permanent conflict between the government, which was supported by the Assembly, and the second chamber of Parliament complicated the political system considerably.

At the end of 1950, the right wing of the enlarged Third Force majority, aided by the violence of the Communists and by their veritable sabotage of parliamentary institutions, persuaded its partners to accept the principle of a partial revision of the constitution in order to return to some of the practices of the Third Republic. This revision was never carried out by the Assembly elected in 1946, however, because of the length of the debates that it devoted to electoral reform. At the time of the passage of the electoral law for the Council of the Republic, as during the debates over the question of constitutional revision, the Socialist party showed less resistance than did the MRP to the pressure placed on them by the Moderates and the Radicals. This is because the MRP, whose political importance is coterminous with the Fourth Republic, was particularly reluctant to return to the political practices and institutions of the prewar period, while the Socialists were basically willing to agree to this on several points.

It must be emphasized that the enlarged Third Force majority, divided on economic, financial, and social problems and, to a lesser extent, on political problems, was also divided on religious grounds. In spite of their defeat in the spring of 1948, the Popular Republicans and the Moderates did not conceal their hopes that it would one day be possible to modify the educational *status quo,* which they regarded as too unfavorable for the Catholic schools.

What enabled parties so badly divided to govern, however tenuously, for almost four years was less their agreement on a positive policy than their persistent refusal to give way to communism and Gaullism. The strikes provoked by the Communists in 1947 and 1948; the insurrectionary and partisan character with which they were marked and which largely contributed to their failure; the Communist demonstrations against French foreign policy, demonstrations which became more and more violent as French policy became more clearly oriented toward agreement with the West on resisting Soviet imperialism; the attempts to sabotage French national defense—in short, everything in the attitude of the Communist party which made it appear again, after the hiatus of the Resistance and of the Liberation, to be a party of demagogic violence and opposition and above all concerned only with defending the interests of the Soviet Union—sufficiently explain why no accord could be reached between it and the parties of the Third Force, even those most interested in defending the proletariat. As to the persistence, and even in one sense the aggravation, of the hostility between the Center majority and the RPF, this is of such importance in tracing the origins of the political situation at the time of the election of June 1951 that it must be studied separately.

The Transformation of the RPF into a Party: November 1947–June 1951

When General de Gaulle created the RPF in the spring of 1947, he did not intend to add one more political party to those among which the French voters were already divided. Quite the contrary, he wanted to create an organization capable of transcending the old divisions of opinion by rallying Frenchmen of all beliefs into a common attempt to accomplish certain objectives essential for the public welfare. In his mind, the word *rassemblement* meant something quite different from the word *party*. Four years later, during the electoral campaign of June 1951, every indication was that the RPF had nevertheless become a party like the others, and even a more disciplined party than most of the groups which, from the

Right Center to the Left, formed electoral coalitions both against it and the Communist party.

General de Gaulle's scheme faced from the start a serious obstacle in the unfavorable reaction of the Socialists and the less unanimous and more qualified opposition of the Popular Republicans. In order to attract the citizens faithful to the traditional, Socialist Left or those sympathetic to the MRP's attempt to synthesize the Right and the Left of earlier days, the RPF had to overcome the handicap presented by the hostility of the political organizations to which these citizens had given their votes in 1945 and 1946. Moreover, Gaullism gave priority among its objectives to the struggle against the "separatism" of the Communists. Except for an infinitesimal number of individual exceptions, the RPF could not count on the support of those Frenchmen who had rallied either earlier or more recently to the new incarnation of the extreme Left tradition which the Communist party represents. These difficulties did not exist in the Center (RGR), and on the Right (PRL, Independents, and Peasants). In addition, these political groups were less disciplined than those of the Left and the extreme Left. They did not try to prevent their members from joining the RPF and therefore placed no obstacles in the way of the RPF's penetration of the sectors of the population whose sentiments, opinions, and interests they represented. It was obvious from the start that the RPF would have great difficulty in transcending the traditional hostility between Left and Right, but it was less difficult for it to combine with the various conservative groups from the PRL to the RGR. This meant strengthening French conservatism by bringing back into its fold the voters who had turned toward the MRP in 1945 and 1946, not because of their convictions, but because of their hostility to communism. On the whole, that is precisely what happened at the municipal elections of October 1947, at least in the cities. But it was difficult for the RPF to consolidate this conservative victory because it could not remain content with it.

General de Gaulle sincerely intended to appeal to every shade of opinion and was sincere in denying that he was interested only in its conservative elements. Although the bulk of the votes cast for lists endorsed by the RPF in October 1947 came from the old Right, some came from proletarian areas which had usually been oriented to the extreme Left. This was a promising omen which permitted the RPF to hope that, despite the opposition of the left-wing parties, it would succeed eventually in winning over at least some of their supporters. In order to accomplish this, it was obviously necessary to adopt a program satisfying the aspirations of the proletariat and, therefore, almost necessarily displeasing to those groups desirous of maintaining the classic capitalistic economy.

In January 1948, in the industrial and mining city of Saint-Etienne, which had just gone over to the RPF thanks to many workers' votes, General de Gaulle delivered a speech devoted to this program. He called for reforms in the organization of industry so that it would have the character of an association between capital and labor, in order to abolish both class antagonisms and the old dependence of the worker on the boss, in order to place them on an equal footing, and in order to substitute for capitalism and its wage system a sort of co-operative system of remuneration.[10] In spite of its lack of precision and the uncertainty of the measures envisaged for bringing it about (the RPF has never said whether it intended to make the association of capital and labor compulsory or whether it intended simply to encourage it by, for example, tax advantages), the program was bound to upset French managerial groups, who were jealous of their authority in their plants. There is no doubt that in many areas in the October 1947 elections management had used its influence and its financial resources for the benefit of Gaullist candidates. By announcing a program designed to enable the RPF to win the support of the workers, De Gaulle ran the risk of alienating some of those people to whom he owed his electoral victory in October. Moderate and Radical political circles were no less disturbed, as they have always been closely linked with business.

[10] See the text of the speech in *L'Année Politique 1948*, p. 324.

This new program, however, did nothing to change the attitudes of the unions, the Socialist party, or the MRP. The principle of the association of capital and labor was unacceptable to the Socialists because it put on one level the more or less distant owners of an enterprise and the people whose daily work makes it prosper, instead of giving the latter a preponderant role. As for the MRP, its own proposal for reforming French industry closely resembled the association of capital and labor although it used different terminology. But its working-class wing, supported by the Christian unions, was already inclined to regard this proposal as too mild. And the party as a whole could not acknowledge the similarity between its program and the RPF's, because it was anxious to remain on good terms with the Socialists by forestalling any suspicions that it would accept a reactionary, corporative, program. It preferred to view the association of capital and labor simply as a fraud. It goes without saying that for the Communists a reform designed to mitigate or even to abolish the class struggle could only meet with implacable hostility. In addition, the RPF's tendency to want to settle all problems of labor relations on the level of the plant disturbed the CFTC, the FO, and the CGT. Even more than the opposition of the parties, the unanimous hostility of the unions was to limit effectively the appeal to the workers of the RPF's position opposing the traditional structure of capitalism.

This aspect of the RPF's program was not, however, the main reason for the increasing difficulties which arose between 1948 and 1951 between the RPF and many of the Moderate and Radical politicians who had been willing in 1947 to participate in electoral coalitions with the RPF. The main reason is the uncompromising and blunt tactics that the RPF tried to impose on them in Parliament. Moderate members of Parliament have always been very jealous of their freedom of action. The RPF wanted the members of its intergroup to follow the tactics prescribed by the RPF's executive council, where they were hardly represented. This could not very well be to their liking. In addition, the RPF's tactics were to maintain an intransigent opposition, which was different from the policy of those Moderates and Radicals who, since January 1947, had decided to co-operate with tripartism in the hope of thereby progressively increasing their influence over public policy. But the RPF refused on principle to collaborate with the parties of the Third Force. According to the RPF, the "regime of parties" established by the constitution of 1946 was inherently condemned to impotence, and the National Assembly had been deprived of its legitimate authority by the results of the municipal elections of 1947. A new Assembly had to be elected by a majority electoral system, and it should undertake to revise the constitution by increasing the authority of the President. The RPF was resolved to maintain its uncompromising attitude as long as these conditions were not fulfilled. It hoped to be able to prevent the Third Force from governing, and to cause a crisis that would be impossible to resolve without taking the RPF's wishes into consideration. The authentic Gaullists continually took this attitude in Parliament. They modified it only rarely: they agreed to ratify the Atlantic Pact of 1949, to vote for measures in December of 1947 and March 1950 aimed at the Communist party and its activities, and to approve the new electoral system for the Council of the Republic in 1948. They could never muster, however, enough Moderates and Radicals to defeat the governments of the enlarged Third Force, even while the latter was being bitterly fought by the Communists.

The RPF's tactics implied that the political, economic, and international difficulties which would inevitably arise during the long period between the anticipated collapse of the Third Force and the RPF's advent to power, could be regarded as insignificant. It revealed a doctrinaire spirit quite different from the pragmatism of many Moderates, and especially of the Radicals, whose sense of the state is not compatible with a long period of systematic opposition. It assumed the absolute impotence of the governments of the Center, and that it would be impossible for the deputies whose aid was necessary to the Socialists and the Popular Republicans in forming a majority to make their views at least partially prevail. It clashed with the experience of the Third Republic, during which the Moderates had been able to play a significant role, not through intransigent opposition and refusal to accept the political system, but through conciliation and support of the existing institutions. Lastly, and this was undoubtedly not the least important consideration which led the Moderates and the Radicals to rebel against the RPF, General de Gaulle's personality and the memory of the way he had governed when he was in office disturbed many of the politicians. They feared that he was incapable of leading a parliamentary government during normal times because of the very qualities—his absolute refusal to agree at home or abroad to compromise over what he considered to be essential, and his absolute confidence in his own judgment—which had enabled him to play such an important role during the war.

The inability of the RPF to find the Moderate and Radical support in Parliament on which it had counted and without which its tactics were doomed to fail led it continually to toughen its attitude and its methods. The RPF's leaders saw that they could impose discipline only on the members of Parliament who had had to abandon their own party in order to rally to Gaullism. Experience revealed that the practice of double membership, on which the RPF had been based at its formation, was a double-edged weapon. The Gaullists of the Radical party, of the UDSR, of the Peasant party, of the Independent group, and of the PRL had not succeeded in orienting the activity of their groups in the direction desired by the RPF, and many of them paid greater heed to the position of their old parties than to that adopted by the intergroup on orders from the secretariat of the RPF. The RPF reached the point where it no longer really counted on the members of Parliament who were not entirely devoted to Gaullism. The role of the intergroups in the two assemblies continually decreased in importance in comparison with the exclusively RPF groups which had been created. One result of these developments

was that it drove away from the RPF those people who had originally joined it with the intention of promoting greater understanding among the parties and who considered that its increased
intransigence was becoming a divisive factor instead. All these
changes did not take place at once, however, and it is useful to
trace their principal stages.

An attempt was made several months after the municipal elections of 1947, in February–March 1948, to bring about an understanding between the RPF and the Third Force for the purpose
of creating a broad union of national parties. The author of this
attempt was René Pleven, the president of the UDSR, who had
served with De Gaulle on the Committee of National Liberation
and in the provisional government. Through press conferences,
speeches, and numerous conversations, he tried to foster a movement in favor of conciliation. Robert Schuman, then Premier, was
careful not to discourage him. Within the MRP and especially in
the Socialist party, reservations were frequently expressed about
the aims of Pleven's scheme. But it definitely failed because Pleven
received no encouragement from the RPF. On the contrary, General de Gaulle continued to demand the immediate dissolution
of the National Assembly, while the main advantage of the *rapprochement* desired by Pleven would have been to avoid the ex-
citement and the loss of time of an electoral campaign and to
guarantee the government a very large majority in Parliament
and in the country. Pleven, seeing that his efforts would fail because of the RPF's refusal to participate, stopped his conciliatory
efforts after a few weeks.

In April 1948, Gabriel Cudenet, the president of the RGR,
stated his opposition to a dissolution in which he saw only an
"element of agitation." Although it did not commit all the members of the RGR, this attitude revealed the desire of the Radicals
to stand apart from the RPF after having exploited it in the fall
for electoral purposes. When, in July 1948, the formation of the
André Marie–Paul Reynaud cabinet clearly demonstrated the
increase in influence of the Radicals and the Moderates, the RPF's

policy of opposition raised still more doubts on the Right and in the Center of the National Assembly. It was at this time that Pierre Montel, a PRL deputy from the Rhône and vice-president of the Gaullist intergroup, resigned from the RPF.

The growing tendency of the RPF to renounce the idea of double membership in favor of becoming a party in the strict sense was emphasized in December by the formation, on the initiative of René Capitant, a member of the UDSR, of the purely RPF Group for Democratic and Social Action, which was joined by several members of the UDSR, Moderates, and former Popular Republicans. At the same time, after the renewal of the Council of the Republic, an RPF Group for Democratic and Republican Action was formed in the second chamber. The discipline of this group was soon going to contrast greatly with the lack of discipline of the intergroup, which was created at the same time and which was twice as large.

In January 1949, Jean Masson, a Radical deputy from Haute-Marne, resigned from the intergroup and declared that the RPF now deserved the criticism of monolithism that it directed at the parties. In June, the UDSR congress, over which René Pleven presided, dealt with the problem of Capitant's deviations by deciding to prohibit its members from remaining members of the RPF. A few weeks later, disputes arose over a local election in Seine-et-Marne. The Gaullist members of Parliament from the department had supported a different candidate than the one named by the RPF's central office, and they were reprimanded for it. Shortly after this incident, Paul Giacobbi, a Radical deputy and one of De Gaulle's former ministers, resigned from the RPF intergroup of which he was the president and said that "the RPF is killing the Rassemblement."

The RGR's break with Gaullism was then just about complete, but the Moderates' break with De Gaulle was not completed until the fall of 1949. At this time, the methodical and persevering organizational activities of the National Center of Independents were crowned by a successful congress. De Gaulle observed with ill humor this reconstitution of a conservative party which might cut into the votes and the membership of the RPF. A few days later he sarcastically remarked that he wondered on whom the self-styled Independents actually depended, an allusion to the rumors that business organizations were supporting financially this reorganization of the old Right.

Both when the Bidault cabinet was formed, and later when the Socialists withdrew from it, the RPF tried to reach an agreement with the MRP, undoubtedly in order to alleviate the effects of the growing tension in its relations with the RGR and the Moderates. The Popular Republicans reacted coldly to these advances, however, and nothing positive resulted from them.

The transformation which had taken place since the spring of 1948 in the RPF's relations with the parties whose activities it had wanted to harmonize and co-ordinate was illustrated most significantly in July 1950, when René Pleven, in the course of the debate which followed the formation of his cabinet, replied to René Capitant, who had reminded him of his conciliatory efforts in the spring of 1948, that in his eyes "the RPF had become an obstacle to the union of the French."

In the fall, Jacques Soustelle, the secretary general of the RPF, speaking of the future elections, said that what was important for the RPF would be less the number of its deputies than their cohesion and their discipline. This was a formula that was obviously inspired by the RPF's disappointment in the members of Parliament who had flirted with it, and who had not followed its orders when they cast their votes in Parliament. This formula also explicitly betrayed the conversion of the old *rassemblement* into a party. One day in the course of the following winter General de Gaulle himself let the expression "our party" slip from his lips when he was talking about the RPF.

The Radical Socialist party drew the logical conclusion from the RPF's evolution by deciding, in the spring of 1951, to prohibit its members from also belonging to the RPF. It was already so alienated from the RPF that this decision did not provoke the resignation of more than two or three members of Parliament whom everyone had for long known were more Gaullist than Radical.

The results of the evolution since 1947 in the structure, methods, and in the very nature of the RPF could have been, however, offset at the time of the election of 1951. The mechanism of the alliance designed to permit the coalition of the majority parties without infringing upon their independence or even mitigating the contradictions of their respective programs could just as well have been used to create a coalition of the RPF, the Moderates, and the RGR. In many cases the latter two groups, preoccupied as they were with defeating not only communism but socialism, would have willingly agreed to ally their lists with those of the Gaullists. Frequently, even the MRP would have joined these alliances, but, despite the entreaties of its potential partners and contrary to the advice of many of its local representatives, the RPF decided to agree only in exceptional cases to make alliances and to go into the electoral battle alone almost everywhere.

This decision gave one advantage to the RPF in that it was not again identified with the Right, an advantage of which the RPF had become aware during the developments from 1948 to 1951. It also enabled the RPF to present itself as a third solution for those people who opposed communism and who wanted something new because of the ineffectiveness of the governments which had succeeded one another since 1946. It permitted it to deny that it participated, as did the parties that it opposed, in jockeying for purely electoral considerations. Finally, it assured the RPF's secretariat that its candidates were completely loyal and would maintain party discipline. This desire for isolation, which was broken, for local reasons, in only twelve districts out of a hundred, ended by giving the RPF the appearance of a closed, monolithic, and rigorously disciplined party, instead of the rallying point for various parties which it was supposed to be when it was created. For this very reason, the Moderates and Radicals who had never supported the Third Force governments were compelled to join with the Third Force parties, at least for electoral purposes, in order to form the alliances on which the new electoral law placed a premium. The pressure that was, perhaps involuntarily, exerted by the RPF because of its electoral isolation contributed to a great extent to bringing together in the elections not only the Socialists, the Popular Republicans, and their allies of the enlarged Third Force majority, but also all those members of the opposition who had refused to accept the rigorous discipline of the RPF and to subordinate everything to General de Gaulle's accession to power.

In outward appearance, the French political situation was thus clarified by the formation of three major groups, two of which, the RPF and the Communist party, opposed a coalition of all the other parties loyal to parliamentary democracy. Actually, the diversity of the programs of the various elements of the third group was going to create after the elections a more confusing and less stable situation than had ever existed between 1946 and 1951.

II

The Electoral Reform of 1951

THE two Constituent Assemblies of 1945 and 1946 were elected according to a system established by the ordinance of August 17, 1945 of the provisional government of General de Gaulle. The provisions of this ordinance, with some slight exceptions, were retained in the law of October 5, 1946, which was adopted by the second Constituent Assembly and which was applied in November 1946 for the election of the first National Assembly under the constitution of 1946. It is essential to understand the technical provisions and political background of this electoral system in order to understand why its modification became a political problem and how this problem was resolved before the election of 1951.

The Electoral System after the Liberation

After the Liberation, the government substituted for the single-member-district system with two ballots (*scrutin uninominal majoritaire à deux tours*), which had been in effect at the time of the fall of the Third Republic, a system of proportional representation requiring a list of candidates for each electoral district—which was the department. The use of the department as the electoral district limited considerably the proportional aspect of the system because of the large number of small departments having only two, three, or four deputies, where the lists of candidates receiving the fewest votes could not be represented. But the most important characteristic of this electoral system was the principle of "the blocked list," which denied the voter both the right to change the order in which the candidates were placed on the lists and the right to erase certain names and substitute for them the names of candidates on other lists. The principle of the blocked list reduced the voter's role to choosing one of the parties, leaving to the executive committees of these parties the choice of the men who would represent them in Parliament. Theoretically, this system was designed to prevent certain undesirable tactics. For example, it prevented one candidate from trying to increase his own chances of being elected by trying to harm the chances of other candidates higher up on the same list. It also would prevent one party from trying to "decapitate" the lists of its opponents, by having a certain number of its followers vote for the candidates in the lowest positions on rival lists in order to elect them instead of their leaders.

Actually, the real purpose of the blocked list was to increase the authority of the parties over the members of Parliament and to reinforce their role in public life. In 1945 and 1946 the Socialists, the Communists, and the Popular Republicans agreed that the decadence of the Third Republic had been caused by its excessive individualism. They thought that democracy had to be "organized" and that this could be done only through strong parties, capable of maintaining strict discipline among their representatives in Parliament. The passage of an electoral law which made the deputies completely dependent on the parties for their re-election seemed to be one of the most effective ways to make individualism disappear from political life.

The adoption of proportional representation was based on more complicated considerations. During the Third Republic proportional representation had been defended both by the parties of the Right and by those of the extreme Left. The Catholic conservatives, once they had lost all hope of winning the support of a majority of the voters, had thought that proportional representation would at least enable them to maintain some representation in Parliament. The Socialists, before 1914, and later the Communists, beginning in 1920, considered proportional representation to be a means by which they could emphasize their originality and safeguard their independence with respect to the bourgeois parties of the Left. These considerations were important for the Socialists and Communists because the electoral system of the Third Republic, with its majority principle and its two ballots, required them to maintain the tradition of "republican discipline" by withdrawing at the second ballot in favor of the left-wing candidate who had the greatest chance of being elected, even when he might come from a bourgeois party hostile to the economic program of its more radical allies. They wanted to escape from this kind of electoral solidarity. Needless to say, all these careful calculations had been camouflaged on all sides by appeals to a so-called principle of justice according to which every political opinion should be represented in Parliament in proportion to its numerical strength in the country.

The Radicals had been hostile to proportional representation as long as they had been the main beneficiaries of the majority principle and the tactics of republican discipline. When this was no longer the case, after the elections of 1936, and after their break with the Marxist parties over economic and financial policy, most of them thought they would be able to regain their independence through proportional representation. At the beginning of 1939 the Chamber of Deputies adopted proportional representation, but the proposal was still awaiting action in the Senate when the Third Republic collapsed. Actually, France had never really experimented with proportional representation. The rather complicated list system applied in 1919 and in 1924 really embodied more of the majority than the proportional system. The adoption of proportional representation in 1945 was a sort of leap into the unknown, difficult to explain only on the basis of the reasons thus far presented.

Fundamentally, there was quite a different purpose behind the action of the provisional government when it decided to elect the Constituent Assembly by proportional representation. The members of the government undoubtedly wanted to take into account the preferences of the parties in the Consultative Assembly. But on other questions, in particular the referendum which accompanied the election of the Constituent Assembly, General de Gaulle did not hesitate to ignore the advice of the Consultative Assembly. If he did not do so in the case of the electoral system, it was really because, amid the uncertainty concerning the respective strength of the various parties in the country in 1945, proportional representation guaranteed that the election would not produce an Assembly dominated by any single party. This guarantee was extremely important for each of the parties because, by assuring each one some minimum representation in Parliament, it maintained the possibility of each one's eventually participating in a coalition government, and thereby preventing one of its opponents from seizing power. In the era of tripartism, which was characterized by the association of the parties which distrusted one another and which collaborated with one another in the government in order to prevent the others from seizing power completely, the mutual insurance of an electoral system based on proportional representation was essential. One is tempted to say that it was the keystone of the whole system.

A majority electoral system with two ballots, the traditional French system, would have certainly created electoral coalitions polarized around communism and anticommunism in 1945 and in 1946. The MRP would not have been able to avoid participating in the anti-Communist coalition, which would have prevented it from later collaborating in the government with the Communists. The Socialists, on the other hand, carried away by the traditions of the union of the Left and of working-class unity, would have had to engage in mutual electoral support with the Communists. That would have condemned them to collaboration with the Communists in Parliament and in the government, and would not have enabled them to rely on the Popular Republicans to prevent their party from being absorbed by the Communist party. Judging by the results of the election of October 1945, this extreme Left coalition might have had an absolute majority in the Constituent Assembly, which justifies the position of those opponents of communism who then saw in proportional representation a way of checking it. It is true that no consideration of this kind was suggested in the discussions over the electoral system which took place in 1945 in the press and in the party congresses. The main arguments that were presented publicly in favor of proportional representation were the references to a so-called electoral justice and to the necessity of counteracting the individualism of the Third Republic. But there can be no doubt that the calculations of the parties weighed the advantages that proportional representation would have in the uncertain political situation of 1945 at least as much as they did its supposed theoretical superiority over other electoral systems.

The Early Criticisms of Proportional Representation

Since 1945, the Radicals had been criticizing proportional representation. Forgetting that in 1939 they had turned to it in the hope of freeing themselves from the clutches of the Popular Front, they returned to their old position and advocated the single-member-district with two ballots. Their kind of party organization, based on a decentralized network of local committees consisting of a few outstanding and influential people, was well adapted to an electoral system based on small electoral districts where personal influences could play an important role. Their familiarity with political maneuvering led them to view without concern the political alliances for the second ballot, for which they were especially well placed by the political position of their party. The history of their party and its attachment to the old tradition of secularism could enable it to form alliances with the Socialists or even the Communists. On the other hand, their opposition to the political and social innovations of the Liberation and their fidelity to the traditional economic system of free enterprise and private initiative made it quite possible for them also to form an alliance, if necessary, with the conservative Right.

The result of the elections of October 21, 1945, was catastrophic for the Radicals, whose parliamentary representation was reduced to about thirty deputies. This defeat was clearly due in part to the electoral system, for the results of the cantonal elections of 1945, held under the single-member-district system with two ballots, had been much less unfortunate for radicalism. The system of proportional representation had encouraged the voters on October 21 to vote for the large parties which had the most chance of winning a large number of seats, and it had prevented, because of the enlarged electoral districts, the personal influence of the Radicals from having its customary effect on the electorate.

The Radicals, therefore, again took up their cry against proportional representation. They were provided with new arguments in favor of returning to the electoral system of the Third Republic when it soon became apparent that the party system made it difficult to form homogeneous governments capable of carrying out a coherent policy and stamped parliamentary life with a rigidity which stemmed from the dominance of a few large monolithic parties. Some Moderates joined them in demanding the revival of one of the fundamental institutions of the old political system. But others, faithful to the position adopted by their predecessors of the Catholic Right, who saw in proportional representation a guarantee against the permanent dominance of left-wing coalitions, remained hostile to the single-member-district system. However, they demanded that the system installed after the Liberation be made more flexible by giving the voter an opportunity to name the men he wanted to represent him, through the practice of ticket-splitting or the preferential vote.

Criticism of proportional representation was futile, however, as long as it came from the minority parties which had no way of compelling the parliamentary majority to give them satisfaction. The rupture of tripartism in the spring of 1947 changed this situation. Having become an indispensable part of the majority, the Radicals now had a way to put pressure on their allies, the Popular Republicans, who were firmly attached to proportional representation, and the Socialists, who were considerably less so. Proof of this was given during the summer, when the electoral law for the municipal elections was discussed. The MRP would have liked to apply proportional representation to the election of the municipal councils in the towns with more than 2,500 inhabitants. The opposition of the Radicals obliged it to agree to raise this figure to 9,000. Moreover, ticket-splitting and preferential voting were introduced into the system for the towns with more than 9,000 inhabitants. In the smaller towns the old majority-list system with two ballots, with complete freedom of choice for the voters, was retained.

The question of the electoral system for the National Assembly was not really raised until after the municipal elections of 1947. At this time, the RPF declared that the National Assembly had lost its authority because the electorate had disavowed the parties which held a majority there, and demanded a change in the electoral system and new elections. The RPF took up strenuously the criticisms of proportional representation made by the Radicals. But it emphasized the connection of proportional representation with the party system and demanded the re-establishment of the free choice of candidates by the voters as the best way to destroy the dangerous authority of the leaders of the major political parties. The fact that proportional representation had been established in 1945 by an ordinance of General de Gaulle in no way diminished the attacks of the RPF against the system. It was justified, the RPF claimed, for the election of a Constituent Assembly which was to exist only for a few months, but it was not justified for a regular parliamentary assembly. It was difficult to understand why this distinction should be made, but the RPF had to find an argument, however debatable, which would enable it to pretend that there was no contradiction between the General's present attitude and his activities when he led the provisional government.

If the RPF joined the Radicals in criticizing proportional representation, it parted with them over the question of which system should replace it. The RPF proposed a majority list system with two ballots. The single-member-district system, because of its small constituencies, emphasizes local considerations and personalities. It is badly adapted to great political campaigns waged on a national scale, and it prevents the presentation of coalition lists, such as those that the RPF had just presented with the Conservatives and the Radicals in the municipal elections, and which had enabled the RPF to win its great victory. The majoritarian-list system with two ballots, on the other hand, would have been perfect for the formation of such lists. These lists would probably win the most votes on the first ballot, and they would be able, even where they had not won an absolute majority of the votes on the first ballot, to attract at the second ballot the votes of people who had earlier voted for the Center parties but whose main desire was to defeat the Communists. In all probability such coalition lists would have been very successful even if they had won only relative majorities, because of the divisions among their opponents.

The very fact that the RPF made electoral reform a prerequisite for the dissolution of the National Assembly led the opponents of a new election to postpone revising the law of October 5, 1946. When the RGR decided in the spring of 1948 to agree to continue the National Assembly until the expiration of its legal term of office, it reduced its pressure on its partners of the enlarged Third Force for the abolition of proportional representation. During the summer, however, the increase in parliamentary sentiment in favor of a majority system became obvious. When the permanent electoral system for the Council of the Republic (which had been elected in 1946 for only two years) had to be decided upon, the government parties, aided in this case by the RPF, established a majority system except in the ten most populous departments, where proportional representation was retained without ticket-splitting or preferential voting. The major reason for this decision had been the desire to reduce the parliamentary representation of the Communist party, whose isolation prevented it from profiting from the majority principle, and which, since the end of 1947, had made several attempts to obstruct and to sabotage the debates both in the National Assembly and in the Council of the Republic. It was this consideration which was also going to persuade the majority in the National Assembly to change the electoral law of 1946.

The Problem of Electoral Reform: 1950–1951

It was inevitable that the problem of electoral reform would reappear on the center of the political scene during the last year of the life of the National Assembly despite the cessation, during 1948 and 1949, of the Radicals' campaign against proportional representation. The proximity of general elections could only incite the advocates of the majority system to make new efforts in behalf of their position.

Above all, it appeared more and more clearly to the parties of the Center majority that maintaining the electoral system of 1946 might be unfavorable for them. The advantages that the system of 1946 gave to the large parties [1] would benefit the two parties of the opposition, the Communist party and the RPF, and harm the four Center groups because of the very fact that there were four of them. The proportional principle itself might result in the election of an ungovernable assembly if each of the two extreme parties won about one-fourth of the votes.

The interests of the government parties lay, therefore, in adopting an electoral system which would permit them, in one way or another, to bolster one another in the balloting. This required giving certain advantages to a group that could win a relative majority, which the Center parties could do by combining their popular vote. Many advocates of proportional representation understood at this time that justice is not the sole virtue desired in an electoral system, and that it is above all essential that it permit the

---

, [1] Because of the small size of so many departments and because of the absence of any provision for utilizing the wasted votes in each department.

formation of a parliamentary majority capable of governing. The goal of an election in a democracy is not only to reflect popular opinion but, primarily, to create a government.

There were other reasons for abandoning proportional representation. Since November 1947, the parliamentary groups of the Communist party had tried to sabotage parliamentary institutions. Regularly defeated when votes were taken, they expressed their opposition by interminable speeches, insults, and sometimes violence, and they employed every technique of parliamentary procedure to delay the debates and to prevent the majority from bringing them to a conclusion. It was clear that the protection of democratic institutions required that such obstacles to their normal operation be removed. The first prerequisite for this was to reduce the number of Communist deputies. It would, of course, have been contrary to the fundamental principle of democracy to abolish the Communist opposition completely. But by reducing it in size only, the Center parties left it with the opportunity of expressing itself, while preventing it from paralyzing the work of the assemblies.

In March 1950, the Bidault government, incited by the multiplication of acts of sabotage committed by members of the Communist party against the transportation and manufacture of materials necessary for national defense, introduced a bill to strengthen the legal weapons against these crimes. The Communists fought this bill with unprecedented violence, and the frequent disturbances they created obliged the National Assembly to adjourn often and for long periods. It was this which persuaded those Popular Republicans who had until then remained absolutely faithful to proportional representation to accept a change in the electoral system.

The parties of the majority—the Socialists, the Popular Republicans, the Radicals, and the Moderates who were sympathetic to the government—and even some of the Moderates and Radicals who were in the opposition but not subservient to the RPF, had no difficulty in agreeing on the goals of a change in the electoral system. These were to reduce the number of deputies of the iso-lated parties, which meant certainly the Communist party and eventually the RPF; to make it possible for neighboring parties to ally with one another; and to introduce the majority principle. The last point was designed to enable a coalition which might win more votes than either of the opposition parties to win a majority of the seats in the Assembly even if the coalition won less than half the total votes cast.

It was much more difficult, however, to reach agreement on the means of accomplishing these goals. The personal interests of cer-tain deputies of the majority, whose re-election was guaranteed under the 1946 law, complicated the problem, and so did mental reservations on the part of the RPF, which recognized the advan-tage it would gain from proportional representation if this system produced an assembly in which there could be no anti-Communist majority without the RPF. The case for proportional representa-tion presented by these advocates was justified in doctrinal and theoretical terms, but its real purpose was to prevent any change at all from being made.

The major problem was that of deciding whether there would be one or two ballots. Most of the French parties did not even stop to consider a simple majority system with one ballot because the Communists might lead the field, even though with a small percentage of the votes, in many districts. For example, if five candidates out of six were each to receive 16 per cent of the votes, the sixth candidate would be elected with only 20 per cent of the votes. There were precisely six major political groups in France: the Communist party, the RPF, the Socialist party, the RGR, the MRP, and the Moderates; and the Communists could count on about one-fifth of the votes in many departments. There-fore, it seemed necessary to return to the traditional French sys-tem of two ballots in which no one could be elected on the first ballot if he had not won more than one-half of the votes. This system would permit each party to try its luck on the first ballot, and then it would make it possible for those parties who wanted to do so to form an alliance, either by some of the parties with-drawing in favor of a single candidate or, if there were a list of candidates, by forming a coalition list. The Popular Republicans, as well as some Moderates, were absolutely opposed to restoring the two-ballot system. The main reason, although it was sometimes unconsciously held, for this opposition was the bitter memory that the Catholics had of the electoral coalitions made by the anticleri-cal parties during the Third Republic. These parties had fre-quently carried the day, but the coalition was cemented only by anticlericalism, since it consisted of Radicals who preached in-dividualism and Socialists who preached collectivism. Actually, the growth of the Communist party and its complete political iso-lation made the restoration of such coalitions quite unlikely. But the MRP feared that the institution of the second ballot would inject new life into the old tradition of union on the Left and that the response of the voters would provoke a *rapprochement* between the Communist party and the other anticlerical par-ties.

The Popular Republicans also pointed out that during the Third Republic the two-ballot system had never permitted the formation of majorities that were coherent enough to guarantee ministerial stability. On the contrary, between the two World Wars, the left-wing majorities elected in 1932 and in 1936 broke up after two years. The MRP thought that the cause of this phe-nomenon was the negative character of the alliances made for the second ballot, at which the voters voted more *against* a certain policy than *for* a common program. This reasoning overlooked the fact that before 1939 there had always been single-member districts. A majority-list system with two ballots would not have had the same consequences because the candidates of the coali-tion lists formed for the second ballot would have been compelled to present the voters with a minimum common program and, especially, because a real solidarity would have been created among the deputies of the various parties who had been elected by the same voters. Nothing like this developed out of the single-member-district system because one candidate who might have withdrawn from the second ballot in favor of another would maintain the hope of beating in a later election the candidate whom he had just helped to elect.

Whatever their validity, such objections did not succeed in shaking the determination of the MRP. The debates during the congress that the MRP held at Nantes in the spring of 1950 proved that the leaders of the party would find it difficult to persuade the militants to give up proportional representation, to which they remained attached out of loyalty to a firm and theoretical conception of electoral justice and because they wanted to maintain at any price the distinctiveness and the independence of Christian Democracy. Moreover, the leaders of the MRP to a large extent shared the latter preoccupation. One of the main motives, confessed privately but not publicly, for the MRP's opposition to a second ballot was the fear that it would be forced to make contradictory alliances in different regions, allying with the conservatives and the RPF where the religious problem was important and with the Socialists where social problems were important, and ultimately losing its unity as a consequence.

When the Pleven cabinet was formed in July 1950, a ministerial office especially created to deal with the problem of electoral reform was given to Paul Giacobbi, the Radical deputy who had abandoned a year earlier the presidency of the RPF intergroup at the National Assembly. Trying to find a compromise between the opponents and advocates of a second ballot, Giacobbi made a suggestion based on a bill that had been presented several years earlier by a conservative deputy, René Coty (who had in the meantime become a senator). He proposed a majority-list system with two ballots, with the special provision that a list would have to win at least 40 per cent of the votes, either on the first ballot or on the second ballot, in order to receive the seats for a given constituency. If no list won 40 per cent of the votes, the seats would be distributed by proportional representation on the basis of the votes cast at the second balloting. The Pleven cabinet submitted a government bill proposing this system in the fall of 1950, but no Popular Republican minister signed it.

The system was designed, however, to quiet some of the MRP's fears. By refusing to participate in coalition lists on the second ballot the MRP would often have been able to make it necessary for proportional representation to be invoked. This would have permitted it to protect its unity and to participate only in alliances of the same political orientation. But the Giacobbi proposal was open to serious criticism because of the provision that only 40 per cent of the votes would have to be won for an entire list to be elected. The abandonment of the traditional absolute majority rule seemed to be too transparent a maneuver. Many Popular Republicans feared that its purpose was to make MRP participation in the Center coalitions unnecessary. Most of all, their largely irrational opposition was directed at the principle of the second ballot itself and could not be lessened simply because the Giacobbi proposal made changes in the way it had operated during the Third Republic. They continued to fear that they would be in a poorer position than their partners when the time came for the formation of coalition lists for the second, and decisive, ballot.

Several months earlier, two Popular Republican deputies, MM. Roques and Tailhade, had introduced a bill proposing a majority electoral system with one ballot founded on the principle of the alliance of lists. The lists were to be presented independently by each party, but the parties would be allowed to announce before the election their desire to form an alliance. When the total number of votes won by several lists that had previously announced their alliance with one another was more than a given percentage of the total vote (55 per cent in the initial proposal), all the seats for the district would be given to this group of parties and distributed among them by proportional representation. If no group of allied parties attained the required percentage, the seats would be distributed by proportional representation among all the competing lists, the allied parties being considered as a single list. This would enable the allied parties to benefit from the advantage that the largest parties receive in small electoral districts because of the incomplete character of the proportional-representation system which was proposed. As in the first case, the seats going to the allied lists would then be distributed among them proportionally. Such a system was obviously advantageous to the parties of the government coalition. It permitted them to combine their votes in order to benefit from the majority principle without forcing them to harmonize their different viewpoints in order to present to the country a single governmental program. This, however, created a serious obstacle to the cohesion of the future majority.

It could also be feared that public opinion would severely criticize an electoral procedure which might give a seat to a list which was allied with others, but which had won considerably fewer votes than an isolated list which would receive no seats. Such a peculiar electoral system, obviously designed to give a special advantage to certain parties to the detriment of others, might seriously weaken the allegiance of the voters to their political institutions. The MRP considered the negotiations that had taken place during the Third Republic in order to produce electoral alliances for the second ballot to be scandalous, but these at least had had the advantage of being based on the number of votes that each party had won on the first ballot and of being submitted for ratification to the voters themselves. Would not the negotiations between parties for the formation of this new kind of alliance lead to maneuvers that would be just as debatable from the moral point of view as the earlier kind? Regardless of these criticisms, it became obvious in the last months of 1950 that the Popular Republicans and a certain number of Moderates, attracted by the advantages that the system of alliances seemed to offer them, would not accept any electoral reform that called for more than one ballot.

The Electoral Law of May 9, 1951

Discussion of the bill for electoral reform began in December 1950 and after many vicissitudes was terminated in May 1951, hardly more than one month before the elections. It took up so much of the National Assembly's time that it was impossible for the Assembly to undertake the constitutional revision of which the necessity had been formally confirmed by resolutions of both houses of Parliament. The disagreement among those who accepted the principle of a majority system about the number of ballots that should be held permitted the opponents of any change to build negative majorities against both of the two possible solutions. The parliamentary aspect of the problem was further complicated by the calculations of certain members of the Center parties, whose personal interests would be well protected if the present electoral law were maintained, as well as by the RPF's preference for the 1946 system over any other except a majority-list system with two ballots.[2] Early in the spring, the Pleven cabinet resigned because it seemed impossible for the Assembly to reach an affirmative decision.

It required all the political skill of Henri Queuille, who returned as Premier, to persuade the National Assembly to pass the bill. He succeeded in doing this because the attachment of his Radical-Socialist colleagues to the single-member system with two ballots, which was ardently demanded at all their congresses, really represented the sentiments of the active party workers more than those of the party leaders. The militants remembered that the era of the great electoral successes of radicalism, in 1902, 1906 and 1910, had coincided with the operation of this electoral system. But the Radical leaders knew that the weakness of their party in many areas made it extremely doubtful that the single-member district would produce any advantages for them. A list system,

[2] See the analysis of this situation in François Goguel, "La situation politique," *Esprit*, April 1951 (translated into English as "Political Parties in France," *World Review*, June 1951).

with the possibilities of coalition that it offers to a party which is small but whose voters are of decisive importance, really corresponded to their interests. They would have preferred two ballots so that coalitions would not have to be made without the knowledge of the exact strength of the various parties and in order to respect a tradition to which they believed their voters were attached. Everything considered, however, the majority system with alliances and with one ballot protected their interests almost as completely as would a list system with two ballots. That is why they eventually supported it.

For the first time in the history of French electoral laws, the law of May 9, 1951, does not apply the same system in all the departments of metropolitan France.[3] The departments of Seine and Seine-et-Oise have a special electoral system. In these two departments, which are very densely populated and almost completely urbanized (except for part of Seine-et-Oise), the law of 1951 for all practical purposes maintained the system of proportional representation. Instead of proportional representation based on the highest average (*la plus forte moyenne*), however, which operated in 1945 and 1946 and which favors the large parties, the proportional system used in these two departments is based on the largest remainder (*le plus fort reste*), which favors the lists with the fewest votes. The Center majority applied this special electoral system in this region only because the two opposition parties, the RPF and the Communist party, are particularly strong in the Paris area. This demonstrates the extent to which the law of May 9, 1951, was inspired by opportunist considerations on the part of the majority parties in the National Assembly, rather than by considerations of what parliamentary democracy means and the necessary conditions for its operation. The electoral system for the rest of France is defined by Article One of the law of May 9, 1951 as a "majority-list system, with the department as the electoral district, with one ballot, with provisions for the alliances of lists,

---

[3] In order not to burden this study with secondary matters, the electoral system used in Algeria and in the overseas departments and territories has been omitted from the discussion.

and with the possibility of ticket-splitting and preferential voting." This is a definition which hardly corresponds to the way the system actually works.

Ticket-splitting gives the voter the opportunity to write on his ballot the names of candidates of different lists. The preferential vote gives him the opportunity to list in his own order of preference the names of the candidates on the ballot, regardless of the way the names are originally placed. Normally, these two practices would require that candidates on the same list be elected in an order corresponding to the total number of votes each candidate received personally. The law of May 9 required, however, that before this could be done, at least half of the printed ballots would have to be modified by the voters, either by ticket-splitting or by expressing preferences. The majority of the voters do not know the candidates well and always vote for the list of candidates of their favorite party just as it is presented to them. The election of June 17 proved that ticket-splitting and preferential voting, as provided for in the law, were really a deception. The order in which the candidates were elected was the same as that in which they appeared on the party lists, and not that resulting from the number of votes that each candidate received individually.[4]

The "majority" aspect of the system is only contingent, and not required. The law provides that all the seats in a district be given either to one party or to a group of allied parties when the average number of votes cast for the party or group of parties is more than half the total. (The 55 per cent requirement of the initial proposal of Roques and Tailhade was not retained because it would have been less favorable to the Center parties.) But when an absolute majority was neither won by a single party,[5] nor by a group of allied parties, the seats were distributed on the

[4] In Loire, M. de Fraissinette, the mayor of Saint-Etienne, who was fourth on the list of National Union (MRP, Independents, UDSR) was not elected on June 17, 1951, although he received personally more votes than the three candidates who preceded him on the list and who were elected.

[5] Actually one list won an absolute majority only in one department, Hautes-Alpes, in June 1951.

basis of proportional representation. Under this system, based on the highest remainder in the Paris area and on the highest average in the rest of France, allied lists were treated as a single list. The law also provides that the allied lists share proportionally the seats that have been won by them, whether on the basis of an absolute majority or proportional representation. The electoral law of May 9, 1951, is thus a combination of the majority and proportional systems, although the first article of its text ignores the second aspect of the system.

One of the major criticisms directed at the 1946 electoral system concerned the excessive authority that it gave the governing organs of the organized parties and the excessive role that these parties played in political life because of it. The law of May 9, 1951, has hardly changed this situation. On the one hand, the provisions for ticket-splitting and preferential voting, which might have been effective ways of reducing the role of the parties in the final choice of successful candidates, were only illusory. On the other hand, the opportunity to form alliances was limited to lists presented by "national parties or groups." To fulfill this requirement, a party or group had to present candidates in at least thirty departments. This was a provision overtly designed to maintain the monopoly of participation in public life that the parties had earlier gained, and to reduce the chances for election of really independent candidates.

Politically, the electoral system which has just been described corresponded directly to the immediate interests of the various Center parties, those which had constantly supported the governments of the enlarged Third Force as well as those which had been, although not subservient to the RPF, generally in the opposition. It enabled them to combine their votes in order to beat their common Gaullist and Communist adversaries without requiring them to make the conciliatory efforts necessary for the elaboration of a single program. For example, it permitted Popular Republicans who advocated subsidies for church schools and anticlerical Socialists to defend contradictory principles and at the same time to benefit from their agreement on the general nature of the political system. The only requirement was that they express this solidarity before election day by a simple declaration of alliance, which committed them in no way to act together in Parliament and which reflected only a temporary identity of electoral interests. Similarly, it enabled Moderate advocates of economic liberalism to ally themselves with the Socialists without obliging either group to make the least effort to harmonize their theoretical concepts or to surmount their antagonism by drafting a realistic program for economic, social, and financial action.

The overt aim of the system of alliances was to protect parliamentary democracy against the two extreme parties which menaced it. Its great fault was obviously that it created among the parties which counted on profiting from it a solidarity that was purely negative. These parties were agreed on opposing the Gaullists and the Communists, but they agreed on nothing positive, not even on the reform of parliamentary procedure, which was just as necessary for protecting the parliamentary system as the existence of a majority in favor of this system. It is clear that the new electoral system does not compel allied parties to agree on a governmental program any more than did the single-member-district system of the Third Republic. It was even less useful for this purpose, for during the Third Republic the awareness that certain candidates would have to withdraw in favor of others at the second ballot obliged the parties to act with a certain amount of restraint during the electoral campaign. Under the new system, once the declaration of alliance is made, each of the parties to it is completely free to emphasize its particular program without affecting the alliance that it has contracted.

The major disadvantage of the system is that it gives the voters the impression that the electoral game is not being played fairly. The genuine majority principle and proportional principle are clear enough for even the most unenlightened members of the public to understand and to accept. This is not true of the hybrid and complicated system of alliances. The combining of the votes received by the allied lists is an abstract operation, done *a posteriori,* which has no basis in reality. It is inevitable that the public should regard the results as unjust, even if it recognizes the effectiveness of the procedure. There you have the germ of skepticism about the honesty of the fundamental machinery of the democratic system which may provoke the alienation of the people from democracy. Certainly, it is the major disadvantage of the electoral law of 1951.

It must be recognized, however, that this law to a large extent corresponded to the necessities of the political situation as it had developed since 1947. There was a disparate majority "condemned to live together" by the pressure of two powerful opposition groups which were violently hostile to each other. The diverse elements of the majority differed on the major problems of economic, social, financial, and religious policy. The basic and most troublesome aspect of the electoral problem was this division of French opinion into several sectors, none of which could gain the support of a clear majority. To this problem the law of May 9, 1951, gave an expedient solution which was more apparent than real.

III

The Elections of June 17, 1951

THEORETICALLY, the National Assembly which was elected for five years on November 10, 1946 should have been replaced in the fall of 1951. At the end of 1950, however, it was recognized that there would be advantages in terminating its mandate several months earlier and in holding elections before the summer. This was a return to the tradition of the Third Republic, when voting in the spring was so firmly fixed as an institution that on two occasions, in 1893 and in 1919, the life of the legislature elected in the fall had been prolonged by several months in order to enable the following elections to be held in the month of May. The reasons for this preference spring essentially from the largely rural character of French society. In the countryside, the winter, the summer, and the fall are not good times in which to hold elections. During the winter, communications are bad, especially in the mountainous areas; during the summer, agricultural work is too intense, and there might be a great many abstentions. During the fall, after the vintage and the harvest are finished, the peasants are often dissatisfied either because the crop is small and they feel that they have worked in vain or because the prices of their overabundant products are fixed at a level that they regard as too low, whether the price is fixed by the law of supply and demand, as in earlier days, or by the government, as it is today. This seasonal bad humor of the rural population quite naturally may

79

be translated into unfavorable votes for the parties in power, and the latter prefer to hold the elections at another time.

On the other hand, Assemblies are always particularly nervous and susceptible to demagogy during the period preceding a general election. The Assembly elected in 1946 was no exception to the rule. At a time when it was believed that it would not be possible to close the fiscal year without voting new taxes, it seemed preferable to advance the date of the election in order not to confront the deputies, who were on the verge of facing their voters, with this unpopular, but necessary, measure. That is why the Queuille cabinet included in its program the passage of a law requiring the National Assembly to adjourn before the summer. After the budget and the electoral law were voted, this proposal was submitted to Parliament, which accepted it without difficulty, and elections were fixed for June 17.

The Electoral Campaign and the Alliances

The electoral law of May 9, 1951 gave great importance to alliances. It very quickly became clear that the RPF would not reverse the position it had taken during the winter and that it would ally its lists with those of the other parties only in exceptional circumstances. The Communists could make no alliances, out of both principle and necessity. The great unknown of the election concerned the alliances that might be made among the parties of the Center. A number of experts on French politics believed that it would be very difficult to get the local militants of the parties to accept the principle of alliances. It was felt that on the local level the parties were separated by too much resentment and discord. Actually, it did not turn out this way. The effectiveness of the system was understood perfectly, and the electoral alliances that the law permitted the parties to make were concluded in many areas. It is interesting to analyze the geographical distribution of the alliances that were made for the election of June 17 (map 1).

In twelve constituencies there were no alliances at all. Six of

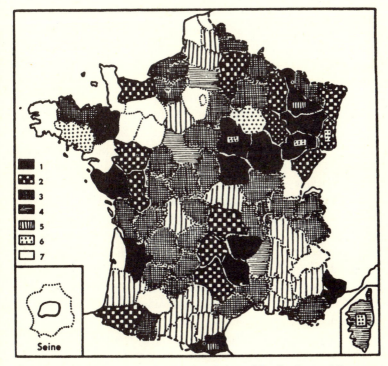

Map 1. Party alliances in the National Assembly elections of June 17, 1951.

1. Alliances between the RPF and other parties.
2. Rightist alliances, without RPF.
3. Alliances from the Right to the Socialists.
4. Alliances from the Right to the Socialists, without full Radical or MRP support.
5. Alliances of MRP, Radicals, and Socialists, without the Right.
6. Alliances of Radicals and Socialists.
7. No alliances.

these constituencies were departments[1] in the west, where the religious question cut off the MRP from its Radical or Socialist colleagues of the Third Force, but where the MRP considered itself to be strong enough to maintain its independence from the

[1] In 1951, just as in 1945 and 1946, the electoral district was the department.

old Right and the RPF. In the first district of Nord, Paul Reynaud had tried to create a broad anti-Communist alliance, from the RPF to the Socialists. He did not succeed and at the last moment decided to enter the electoral battle alone; as a consequence, a projected MRP-Socialist alliance collapsed. Elsewhere, in the first district of Pas-de-Calais, the first district of Gironde, in Jura and in Gers, alliances among the parties of the Center were prevented mainly by personality difficulties. In Gers, for example, the Socialists refused the alliance proposed among them, the Radicals, and the MRP because of the first candidate on the Radical list, Abel Gardey, a former senator who had opposed the Popular Front from 1936 to 1938 and who had voted to delegate powers to Pétain in 1940. In Hautes-Alpes, there were no alliances because the parties of the Center, from the Moderates to the Socialists, agreed to present only one coalition list consisting of an Independent, Maurice Petsche, and a Popular Republican. In brief, outside the six western departments, the absence of alliances had practically no political significance and was due to strictly local considerations.

The RPF concluded alliances in only thirteen districts, six of which were in northeastern France, where the MRP had penetrated only slightly in 1945 and 1946, and where the Right was too powerful for the RPF to fight it with any real chance of success. These alliances linked the RPF with the Right, and with the MRP in Haute-Saône (where it was a question of ending the domination of the department by a Radical deputy of Corsican origin and of dictatorial habits, M. Maroselli). In Alpes-Maritimes, the RPF allied itself with the RGR list and an Independent Socialist list in order to eliminate Communist representation completely in this department. The leaders of the RPF opposed this alliance, which was negotiated by the candidate at the top of the RPF's

---

However, the most populous departments were divided into several districts: six for Seine, three for Nord, two for Pas-de-Calais, Seine-Inférieure, Rhône, and Bouches-du-Rhône. In 1951 Gironde was added to the list of divided departments.

list, General Corniglion-Molinier, but the latter succeeded in maintaining it thanks to his personal friendship with General de Gaulle. In Lozère and Haute-Loire, the RPF was quite weak and allied with the MRP and the Moderates because it did not want to divide the Catholic vote. The same consideration explains the alliance of the RPF with the MRP in Vendée. In this department it was Monsignor Cazaux, the Bishop of Luçon, who was very influential with the peasant voters and the leader of the agitation in favor of state aid for private schools, who induced the RPF and the MRP to make this alliance. In one other western department, Ille-et-Vilaine, the RPF opposed the MRP list of Pierre Henri Teitgen by allying itself with the Independent list of Guy La Chambre, who had been mayor of Saint-Malo since 1947 under the Gaullist label, but who had formed a special list for the legislative election. In this case, the alliance reflected the common hostility of the Moderates, whether they were Catholics or not—La Chambre had been a Radical deputy during the Third Republic—toward the social program of Christian Democracy. In the rural district of Gironde, the strength of the right-wing Independent and Peasant list attracted the RPF, which was concerned with beating not only the Communists but also the Socialists.

In the traditionally conservative departments of the west (at least those where no alliances were concluded), the east, the Massif Central, and the western Pyrénées, the alliances were clearly oriented to the Right on a religious basis and united the Moderates with the MRP, to the exclusion of all the anticlerical parties. (In Aveyron and Cantal, where the Radicals joined these Catholic alliances, it was because of their deep hostility to socialism.) Under these circumstances, "clerical" alliances were sometimes opposed to "anticlerical" alliances of Radicals and Socialists.

In a large part of the southeast and southwest, the alliances united the Socialists, Popular Republicans, and Radicals against the Right. In these areas the Right was so weak that an alliance with it seemed to be dangerous; an agreement with it might have lost more votes for the Third Force parties than they would gain from its support.

In four departments, Oise, Loir-et-Cher, Ardèche, and Corsica, local difficulties produced alliances that were only partial among the Center parties. In Oise the Socialists were excluded, as well as one of the two RGR lists; in Loir-et-Cher and Ardèche the Radical lists were excluded; and in Corsica the MRP presented no candidates.

Everywhere else, or in about one-third of the constituencies, general alliances were concluded among Moderates, Radicals, Popular Republicans and Socialists. In most cases, these alliances were made in departments where the religious question was of little political importance and where the major concern of the four groups and their voters was to beat the Communists. In Moselle, Robert Schuman, and in Côtes-du-Nord, René Pleven, were able, thanks to their personal prestige, to lead this alliance of Center parties to victory in spite of the existence of a great deal of antagonism between Catholics and anticlericals.

In some cases, several parties pooled their efforts by presenting a single coalition list of candidates representing different political groups. In Corrèze, Henri Queuille, the Premier, headed a joint list presented by the Radicals, Socialists, and MRP, which was allied with an Independent list. In Loire, three ministers in the Queuille cabinet, Bidault, Pinay, and Claudius Petit, were candidates on a single list of National Union sponsored by the MRP, the Independents, and the UDSR, and this list was allied to another coalition list sponsored by the Radicals and Socialists. In Moselle, Robert Schuman, the Minister of Foreign Affairs, ran on a joint list with Independent candidates; and in the Morbihan, the Independents and the MRP also presented a joint list. In Vendée, the Socialists and the Radicals joined forces (unsuccessfully) against the Catholic alliance of the MRP and the RPF. In three departments, Eure-et-Loir, Loire-Inférieure, and Vendée, the RPF list contained the names of Independent deputies running for re-election. Radicals and Independents presented joint lists in several areas like Jura, the constituency of Edgar Faure, the Minister of the Budget; Côtes-du-Nord, where René Pleven, then Vice-Premier, was running for re-election; and Meuse, the district of Jacquinot, the Minister of Veterans' Affairs.

As a whole, co-operation between parties took the form of alliances much more frequently than that of coalition lists. The formation of a joint list leads to many difficulties over how many places should be allowed for each party and the order in which the candidates are to be placed on the list. Because in June 1951 there was only one ballot, the parties were not able to judge with precision how many voters could be expected to vote for the list, as they had been able to do during the Third Republic, when coalitions could be formed between the first and second ballots. It is significant that coalition lists were formed for the June elections mostly where there was an important minister who was, as a matter of course, placed at the head of the list of candidates. In the majority of cases, the contradictory claims of the parties could not be reconciled, and the technique of the alliance was far preferable to the formation of a coalition list.

The disadvantages of the system of alliances became very clear during the electoral campaign. The programs of the Center parties differed greatly. Their only common feature was a decisive anti-communism, but their attitudes toward the RPF were much less consistent. The two parties which spoke out most vigorously against any thought of reconciliation with Gaullism were the Socialists and the Radical-Socialists of the Herriot variety, who were attached to the idea of an agreement between the Radicals and Socialists in order to revive under the Fourth Republic the old "Union of the Left" of the Third Republic. In most of the departments the right-wing Independents and Peasants were much more cautious concerning the RPF. They were content with expressing regret over the stubborn way in which the RPF had preferred to run the risk of seeing Communists elected rather than form alliances with other parties. This was also the attitude of the Radical-Socialists of the Daladier type and of most of the candidates who declared their allegiance to the RGR rather than to the parties of which the RGR was composed.

One of the important features of the electoral campaign of 1951 was the obvious divergence of views between the Radical party and the RGR. The followers of Herriot emphasized their ties with the Socialists, while the followers of Daladier emphasized their affinity with the Independents and Peasants. Some went so far as to speak of a "Fourth Force," consisting of the Moderates and the RGR, and characterized by an attachment to the parliamentary system (which would distinguish it from the RPF), by an attachment to orthodox liberal solutions of economic problems, and by hostility to the nationalization of industries and the extension of the social-security system which were carried out after the Liberation.

The MRP generally adopted an attitude of reserve toward the RPF, although it did not condemn the RPF as categorically as the Socialists did. It did not reject in advance the eventuality of an agreement with the Gaullists, but it was careful to indicate that any such development would have to be based on certain conditions and that there would have to be complete equality among the participants in any such agreement. In other words, the Popular Republicans did not want to submit to any RPF ultimatum, because they refused to disavow the Third Force and to accept any guilt for their behavior since 1946. On the other hand, they were careful not to identify Gaullism with neo-Fascism, as their Socialist allies did.

It must be emphasized that all the non-Communist parties, the RPF included, were unanimous in approving the principles of the foreign policy followed by the Third Force governments and in recognizing the necessity for the rearmament undertaken by the powers of the Atlantic Community. This unanimity however, did not prevent some Socialist and MRP candidates, as well as the entire RPF, from stating that it was necessary for France to make her voice heard in the interallied councils of the Atlantic Pact much more than had until then been the case, as well as to prevent an agreement between equals from becoming, *de facto* or *de jure,* an alliance in which the weaker partners would be subordinated to the United States.

Contrary to what had happened in 1946, the question of the legal status of the Catholic schools was raised by the RPF, the Independents, the MRP, and, in two or three departments, by the RGR. These groups all insisted that the Catholic schools should be aided by public funds. On the other hand, the orthodox Radicals and the Socialists declared their fidelity to the traditional idea of the separation of state and church, which precluded such subsidies. Naturally, the Communists tried to exploit this dissension between allied parties in order to win the support of the anticlerical voters. The Socialists who wanted to win over some of the working-class voters of the Communist party, included in their program the demand for a sliding wage scale, undaunted by the objections of the liberals of the Fourth Force, and even of the Popular Republicans, who regarded this measure as inflationary. The allied parties, from the Right Center to the Left Center, did not defend a coherent governmental program before the voters except on foreign policy and on their common attachment to the parliamentary system. Even concerning the latter question, they felt that constitutional changes were necessary, although they did not state precisely what changes should be made. They were agreed on what they did not want—the complete seizure of power by the Gaullists or by the Communists—but they obviously differed on economic matters and even on the political methods by which their coalition might be able to overcome the dangers against which it had been erected. None of them dared to defend without reservation the coalition governments which had succeeded one another since 1947.

One of the most striking features revealed by the electoral campaign of 1951 was the reorganization of the conservative forces of the old Right. The organizational efforts of the National Center of Independents succeeded in creating before the elections a National Union of Independents, Peasants and Republicans, which was a federation of the Peasant party, the PRL, and the Independents. This union, the IPRN, actually was a more unified conservative bloc than the Moderates had been able, until then, to form. There were dissident conservative lists presented to the voters also. Two "national organizations," within the meaning of the law of May 9, 1951, were formed during the electoral campaign: the Taxpayers Defense Group (Groupement National de Défense des Contribuables et des Libertés Professionelles) and the Rally of French Republican and Independent Groups (RGRIF). The former seems to have been inspired to a large extent by the National Organization of Small and Medium Businesses which, since the Liberation, had led a very active campaign against *dirigisme,* against the social security burdens of the employers, and against taxes. The Taxpayers Defense lists frequently refused to make any alliances, undoubtedly hoping to benefit from the preference for isolated lists which it was expected the voters would show. Actually, events proved that the voters were much more interested in making their votes count. The Taxpayers Defense list won very few votes, and only one of its candidates was elected, M. Bessac, an MRP deputy from Lot whose party no longer wanted him as a candidate.

The RGRIF lists, on the contrary, formed alliances almost everywhere. Actually, this was a fictitious party created in order to permit all kinds of diverse groups ranging from *pétainistes* to Independent Socialists to participate in local alliances, as they could do so only if they belonged to a "national organization" endorsing at least thirty lists of candidates. The group bearing the title National Unity of Republican Independents (UNIR) consisted of avowed *pétainistes.* It did not succeed in forming thirty lists and elected only three of its candidates, in Seine, Calvados, and Oran.

If the Moderates were successful in becoming unified, such was not the case with the RGR. Not only did its candidates defend contradictory programs in different areas, as has been indicated above, but in certain departments purely RGR lists competed with orthodox Radical-Socialist lists. The UDSR presented some independent lists, but most of them withdrew before the balloting.

The MRP was divided also, but in outward appearance only. It provoked the creation of a National Group of Democratic Republicans which endorsed, sometimes alone, sometimes with the MRP, a certain number of lists led by MRP deputies. But this was only a precaution against the accusation of clericalism in departments where Catholicism was not very strong, as well as a way of giving party lists the appearance of coalition lists. During the electoral campaign, the semi-official organ of the Holy See, *L'Osservatore Romano,* published an article that was very favorable to the MRP. This approbation of the Vatican certainly benefited the MRP in the Catholic departments of the west, of the Massif Central, and of Alsace, as well as in the north. But it was a double-edged blade which could damage the MRP in traditionally anticlerical areas. The label "Group of Democratic Republicans" helped remove this risk.

In some departments, especially in all the districts of the Parisian area, neutralist lists, non-Communist but hostile to the Atlantic Pact, were presented to the voters. In Meurthe-et-Moselle and Hérault, they were led by deputies who had been expelled from the MRP for having refused to ratify the Atlantic Pact, Abbé Pierre and Paul Boulet. They received so few votes that it can be said that they did not represent a significant sector of French opinion.

Although there was diversity in the alliances, which linked different parties in different regions, and although there was an apparent abundance of "national political organizations," there were six major political groups competing during the electoral campaign of May and June of 1951. Two were opposition parties, the Communist party and the RPF. There were four others which were more or less united and more or less in favor of the policies followed since 1947: the old Right, consisting of the IPRN and the small dissident right-wing groups; the RGR, whose members' staunch individualism explains its disparate nature; the Christian Democracy of the MRP; and socialism. It is the public's response to each of these groups which will next be analyzed.

The Electoral Returns

Contrary to the expectations of some observers of French political life, the election [2] of June 17, 1951 was marked neither by

Table *1*. Comparison of election results in 1946 and 1951.

	November 10, 1946		June 17, 1951	
	Votes	%	*Votes*	%
Registered voters *	25,083,000	100	24,522,000	100
Abstentions	5,505,000	21.9	4,861,000	19.8
Communist party	5,431,000	21.6	4,934,000	20.1
RPF	—	—	4,266,000	17.3
Moderates	3,073,000	12	2,295,000	9.3
RGR	2,136,000	8.5	1,980,000	8
MRP	4,989,000	19.9	2,454,000	10
Socialist party	3,434,000	13.7	2,784,000	11.3
Miscellaneous, including Neutralists in 1951	155,000	0.6	239,000	0.9

* The table is based on statistics compiled by the author on the basis of the official results, as they appear in the election reports, prepared for the verification of the credentials of the newly elected deputies by the National Assembly and published in the *Journal Officiel*. These statistics are quite different from those published by the Minister of the Interior immediately after the election. They are more accurate, as those of the Ministry were announced before the verified results were known. The latter are determined in each district three days after the election by an official committee of verification.

The difference between the total number of votes cast and the total of all the votes received by the parties, 709,000 votes, represents the number of blank and void ballots, and the votes lost by voters who struck out certain names on their ballots without replacing them with others, reducing the sum of the average votes received by the various lists (on which the table is based) below the total number of valid ballots.

Also, the decrease in the number of registered voters between 1946 and 1951 is due to the revision of the electoral rolls, which was carried out by modern machine methods, and which revealed that the old rolls in several towns contained a large number of names that were listed more than once.

[2] This study deals only with metropolitan France and not with Algeria, the overseas departments (Réunion, Guiana, Guadeloupe, Martinique), and the overseas territories, where the elections often take place in circumstances which render the conclusions useless that might be drawn from a study of the num-

overwhelming changes in the relative strength of the various parties nor by a particularly large number of abstentions. Table 1 shows in both absolute figures and percentages the results of the election of June 17 in metropolitan France, compared with those of November 10, 1946.

First of all, the two opposition parties, the RPF and the Communist party, received 9,200,000 votes, compared with 9,513,000 votes received by the four allied parties. In other words, the electorate resisted the attraction of the extremes and approved, by a small but uncontestable majority, the parties which can be loosely called the Center parties. There was no electoral tidal wave comparable to the one which had carried the RPF to victory in the large cities in October 1947.

One may make a somewhat artificial calculation and try to measure the electoral results of 1951 in terms of the major line of political demarcation of the Third Republic, that is, the attitude of the parties on the religious question. This reveals that the advocates of subsidies to the private schools (RPF, MRP, Moderates) won 9,015,000 votes compared with 9,698,000 votes won by the opponents of subsidies (RGR, Socialists, Communist party). Taking into consideration the increase in the electorate due to the establishment of woman suffrage, this gap of 683,000 votes is about the same size as those which ordinarily appeared during the Third Republic when a general election was fought over the religious question. In 1902, for example, advocates and enemies of the secular policy of Waldeck-Rousseau had been separated by a gap of 400,000 votes.

But in 1951 the RGR was not unanimous in opposing subsidies. Some members of the UDSR and even of the Radical-Socialist party explicitly stated that they favored them. In addition, conservative and Catholic voters cast their ballots for the RGR in departments where there were no Independent candidates who

---

ber of votes received by each party. In the following section, however, which deals with the number of deputies elected by each party, the overseas deputies will be taken into consideration.

had any real chance to be elected. It is therefore possible that, in
reality, there was in the electorate of 1951 a small majority in
favor of subsidies. A public opinion poll taken by the Institut
Français d'Opinion Publique [3] in October 1951 showed the following results: 45 per cent for subsidies; 42 per cent against; 13 per
cent without opinion. The majority in favor of subsidies is due to
women, of whom 49 per cent are for and 36 per cent against, while
42 per cent of the men are for and 47 per cent against. It seems
that one can conclude that if the majority position on this issue
is different from that of the Third Republic, it is due to a large
extent to the establishment of woman suffrage. There is nothing
surprising in this, for it is known that for a long time there have
been more girls than boys in the Catholic schools and that the
practice of Catholicism is more widespread among women than
among men.

It cannot be claimed either that the results of the election of
June 17 formally condemned the reforms enacted at the time of
the Liberation by the former tripartite majority. The elements of
this majority—Popular Republicans, Socialists and Communists
—received 10,172,000 votes, compared with 8,541,000 won by the
other parties, including the RPF.

The election of June 17, 1951, therefore, was distinguished by
no decisive shift in opinion either from what it had been during
the Third Republic or from what it had been during the first
years of the Fourth. One must, however, point out the constant
reduction, from October 1945 to June 1951, in the percentage of
votes received by the two Marxist parties, the Communist party
and the Socialist party: from 38.8 per cent in October 1945, this
percentage declined to 35.5 per cent in November 1946. It was
only 31.4 per cent in June 1951, which almost brings it down to
its 1936 level of 28.9 per cent. In this sense, one can say that the
election of 1951 was marked by a rather pronounced movement
to the Right, the majority of the voters appearing to be definitely
opposed to the principle of a collectivist economy, although there

---

[3] Published in Le Figaro, Oct. 18, 1951.

was no majority in favor of an orthodox liberal economy either.

The percentage of the electorate which abstained (19.8 per cent) was greater than the customary pre-war level (17 per cent in 1924, 15 per cent in 1936) and even than that of the referendum of May 5, 1946 (18.1 per cent), but it was smaller than that of November 10, 1946 (21.6 per cent). The noncommunist press had waged a vigorous campaign against abstaining by declaring that to abstain would be to help elect the Communists. This campaign bore fruit, in spite of the discouragement and the wide dissatisfaction with the political system that political developments since the Liberation had undoubtedly created in the minds of many voters. The reduction in the number of abstentions would seem to reflect, at least in part, the hostility of four-fifths of the French people toward communism.

The geographical distribution of the abstainers (map 2) reveals nothing new. As always, the department of Nord, augmented by the mining district of Pas-de-Calais, is the one with the fewest abstentions. Northern France in general, from the Belgian frontier to the Seine River, and the Paris area form the largest region where there were few abstentions. The urban areas generally have fewer abstentions than the rural areas, although there are some exceptions which cannot be easily explained; for example, there are more abstentions in the districts which include Lyons and Bordeaux than in the neighboring countryside. There are more abstentions in sparsely populated regions and mountainous areas than in densely populated, level districts, but the material difficulties which sometimes prevent people from voting in sparsely populated or mountainous areas can be counteracted by religious fervor. The bishops really make it a duty of their followers not to abstain, and this is why, although the regions are basically similar, people in the west vote more often than the people in the southwest, and the people in the southern part of the Massif Central vote more frequently than do those of Auvergne. Sometimes, as in Corrèze, where Premier Henri Queuille was at the head of a coalition list presented by the Radicals, the MRP, and the So-

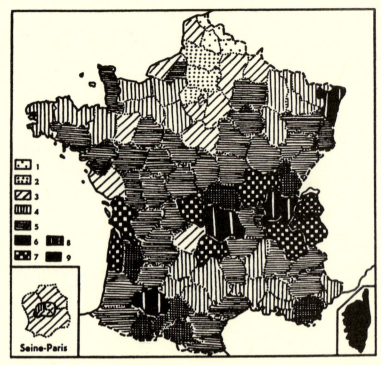

Map 2. Abstentions (per cent of registered voters) in the National Assembly elections of June 17, 1951.

1. From 10 to 12.5 per cent.
2. From 12.5 to 15 per cent.
3. From 15 to 17.5 per cent.
4. From 17.5 to 20 per cent.
5. From 20 to 22.5 per cent.
6. From 22.5 to 25 per cent.
7. From 25 to 27.5 per cent.
8. From 27.5 to 30 per cent.
9. More than 30 per cent.

cialists, the small number of abstentions can be explained by the intensity of the election campaign and the interest aroused by the personalities of the candidates.

The results of the election will now be examined, party by party, both from the point of view of the number of votes each party received in the country as a whole and from the point of view of the geographical distribution of these votes.

The Communist party, which received almost 5,000,000 votes, won more votes than any other party on June 17, just as it had on November 10, 1946. But four out of every five Frenchmen, if one takes into account the total number of registered voters, and three out of every four, if one considers only those who actually voted, persist in not voting for the Communists. The Communist party has not only failed to gain votes since 1946, but it has lost some, about half a million, or 9 per cent of the votes it had received at the preceding election. Moreover, it did not win an absolute majority in any electoral district.

The geographical distribution of the Communist vote (map 3) reveals three main areas of strength and three main areas of weakness.

The zones of strength are in northern France (including the Paris area), in central France, and in the Mediterranean southeast. Only the first of these three areas is characterized by a large industrial proletariat. Central France is purely rural, and the southeast is more rural than industrial. These two bastions of communism always voted for the extreme Left during the Third Republic, first for the Radical Republicans, then for the Radical-Socialists, later for the Socialists; now they vote for the Communists. The latter are the beneficiaries of an old and peculiar political tradition. It is likely that many of their voters share the sentiments of the Communist mayor of a rural town in the southeast who told one of the author's friends, three or four years ago, that if he voted for the Communist party it was certainly not so that it could take power! The explanation of this paradox can be found in the very old French attitude of hostility to the state, which undoubtedly goes back to the days of Richelieu, when the monarchy became powerful and centralized, and in the desire to weaken as much as possible a government that is assumed in advance to be reactionary by strengthening those parties which can thwart it or paralyze it. The purpose of those people who vote for the extreme Left in this spirit is to weaken the state and to prevent it from intervening in their affairs. The more farsighted of

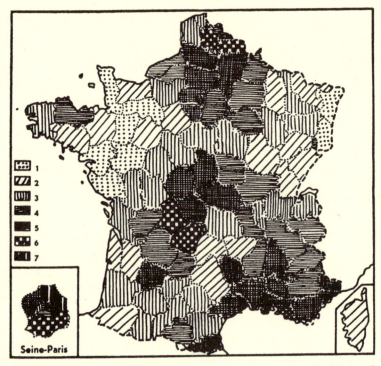

Map 3. Communist votes (per cent of registered voters) in the National
Assembly elections of June 17, 1951.

1. From 5 to 10 per cent.
2. From 10 to 15 per cent.
3. From 15 to 20 per cent.
4. From 20 to 25 per cent.
5. From 25 to 30 per cent.
6. From 30 to 35 per cent.
7. From 35 to 40 per cent.

these people feel some concern over the possible conquest of power
by the party for which they vote, for they can hardly expect that
that party would not employ vigorously the means of action which
would fall into its hands. But the tradition of voting for the candidate who is farthest to the Left still remains strong, and the
true nature of communism, which is so inherently different from
the old parties of the Left of which it is the heir, is not sufficiently
understood by the mass of voters for them to turn away from the

party whose triumph would produce consequences which they do not at all want.

In northern France and in the Paris area, the factors which explain the Communist vote are quite different. These are areas where the economic structure, both industrial and agricultural, is very modern and where a large proletariat leads its entire life,. both during working and leisure hours, within a collective framework. The desire of this group of people to extend collectivism is quite natural. Why their desire should be expressed by a resolute opposition movement and by votes for communism is explained by the inadequate standard of living of this proletariat. To give only one example, the three districts of Paris where the Communist party received the largest percentage of votes in June 1951, the thirteenth, nineteenth, and twentieth arrondissements, are just those districts which have the worst housing facilities.[4]

A geographical and social analysis, therefore, seems to demonstrate that the factors explaining the strength of communism in France are very diverse, and that its electorate is heterogeneous. This could eventually become an element of weakness for the Communist party. It must be noted, however, that its members who hold electoral office and who represent the areas where individualism is strong have in no way shown any less discipline than those who represent the modern industrial areas.

The main areas where communism is weak are in the west, in the east, and from the south of the Massif Central toward the southwestern Gascon region. The first and third areas are mainly rural and of great Catholic strength (except in Gascony). The second area, which is also strongly Catholic, is much more industrialized. The patriotic and military tradition which stems from the proximity of the frontier, and the desire for order and the civic sense of the people of the east, undoubtedly explain why the growth of

[4] See François Goguel, "Structure sociale et répartition des votes à Paris dans les elections du 17 Juin 1951," *Revue Française de Science Politique,* July–September 1951.

a large industrial proletariat has not been followed by a growth in the Communist vote equivalent to what it is in the north.

Map 4 shows where the Communist party has suffered its greatest losses since November 1946. These losses are unequally distributed throughout various regions and, although the Communists lost votes in the country as a whole, they have made some local gains in certain places. The areas in which they made these gains are all situated in the heart of the oldest Communist bastions: Nord, Pas-de-Calais, and Somme in northern France; Allier, Creuse, Corrèze, Indre, Haute-Vienne in central France; Gard, Drôme, Isère, Hautes-Alpes in the southeast. They made much progress also in Tarn and Garonne, but these are departments in the southwest, where the Communists were weakest in 1946, and the progress there only brought them up to the level of neighboring departments. The gains made in Landes are so slight that they can almost be disregarded.

The areas where the Communist party has most declined in strength (a loss of more than 18 per cent in twenty departments) are where the Moderates or Radicals had generally been strong, but where the Communists penetrated in 1945 and 1946 because of the favorable situation that was created for them by Vichy's propaganda identifying them with the Resistance. The Communists lost this earlier advantage because of their attitude since 1947 and they lost votes. The Communists have also lost sizable numbers of votes in Paris and its industrial suburbs. They are weaker here than they were in 1936. The reasons for this decline are undoubtedly similar to the ones just stated. If they had greater effect in the Paris area than in Nord, Pas-de-Calais, and Somme, it is undoubtedly due to the special psychology of the Parisian population, which is idealistic, acutely aware of the significance of the policies of the various parties, and keenly patriotic. But it is beyond question that the activities of the RPF in the capital and the audience it has won for itself have also played a large role in the Communists' defeat.

Everything considered, the decline of communism in 1951 has altered the uniform geographical distribution of its strength which

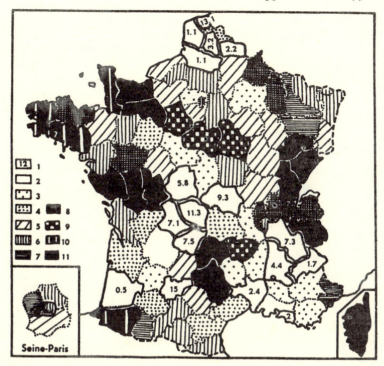

Map 4. Changes in Communist votes between November 10, 1946 and
June 17, 1951.

1. Increase (figures in the map indicate the percentage increase) .
2. No change.
3. Decrease of less than 3 per cent of
   the 1946 percentage.
4. Decrease of 3 to 6 per cent.
5. Decrease of 6 to 9 per cent.

6. Decrease of 9 to 12 per cent.
7. Decrease of 12 to 15 per cent.
8. Decrease of 15 to 18 per cent.
9. Decrease of 18 to 21 per cent.
10. Decrease of 21 to 24 per cent.
11. Decrease of more than 24 per cent.

was revealed in 1946. It remains, however, the only French party
which nowhere receives the votes of fewer than 5 per cent of the
registered voters, just as it is the party which most often receives
more than 30 per cent of the votes. It is clear that in the present
state of the French social structure the Communists can hardly
expect to make any further progress. There is a saturation point

beyond which communism cannot penetrate. But the party's decline has been serious only in those areas which it had only recently penetrated and where it was, therefore, not firmly rooted. Before the strength of the Communists declines in the industrial north, there will have to be a real and enduring increase in the standard of living of the workers. Before the Communists decline in central and southeastern France, the rural population of these areas will have to become aware of the true nature of the Communist party, which is a totalitarian party, alien to the French democratic tradition in its doctrine and its methods. At the present time, the people of these areas are not equipped to understand this.

The second opposition party, the RPF, received more votes than any one of the Center parties, but it did not win as many votes as the Communists did, although it had outdistanced the Communists in the municipal elections of 1947 (in the cities) and in the cantonal elections of 1949. Although no exact comparison can be made, since the RPF did not exist in 1946, it is beyond doubt that the June 1951 election represented something of a setback for the RPF. This setback can easily be explained by the transformation which the RPF underwent in the intervening years. In 1947, and even in 1949, the RPF was still not a party, and it could count as its own votes received by a coalition which included Moderates and Radicals as well as its own candidates. In 1951, it entered the electoral battle alone, forming coalitions with the Independents only in Eure-et-Loir and Vendée and refusing in 90 per cent of the constituencies to participate in the anti-Communist alliances. It is beyond doubt that this isolation caused the Gaullists to lose the votes of many people who wanted more than anything else to defeat the Communist candidates and who preferred for this reason to vote for the allied lists, even though they might have really favored the RPF.

The geographical centers of the RPF's strength (map 5) are mainly in the areas which have been traditionally sympathetic to the Right—the west and the east. But Gaullism does not occupy all the old conservative areas: part of the west and, especially, the

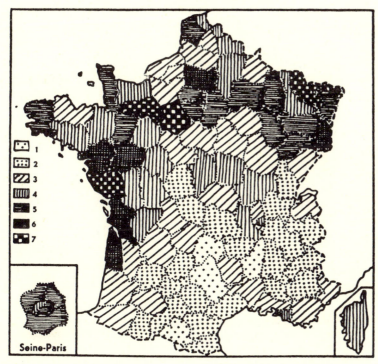

Map 5. RPF votes (per cent of registered voters) in the National Assembly elections of June 17, 1951.

1. Less than 5 per cent.
2. From 5 to 10 per cent.
3. From 10 to 15 per cent.
4. From 15 to 20 per cent.

5. From 20 to 25 per cent.
6. From 25 to 30 per cent.
7. From 30 to 35 per cent.

southern part of the Massif Central, the area north of the Alps, and the area west of the Pyrenees have remained aloof from it. On the other hand, it has penetrated areas that were formerly Radical or Socialist, like Charente-Maritime, Gironde, Marne, and the Paris region. Detailed analyses of the balloting prove that its gains at the expense of the old Left are also noteworthy in Indre-et-Loire, Loire, Rhône, Alsace, Nord, and Ardennes. In Paris and its suburbs, in Lyons, in Nantes, and in Marseilles, it is definitely stronger in the working-class districts than in the middle and upper-class residential areas. A geographical and social analysis therefore demonstrates that it would be erroneous purely and simply to identify the RPF with the old Right. The areas of influence of the two groups are in part identical, but Gaullism is not all of the Right and it is something else besides the Right, just as communism is not the whole working class and is something else as well. With respect to social status and former political affiliation, the RPF's electorate seems to be very diversified. In this sense, Gaullism is certainly a *rassemblement*.

This is not the case from the geographical viewpoint, however. The RPF is really strong only in the cities and the areas which are characterized by a modern economic structure, although the voters' urgent desire to beat the Communists caused the RPF to lose votes in similar areas in the south. In the countryside, it has been successful only where it was able to benefit from a tradition of patriotism and the desire for a strong state, as in the east, and where the local leaders of the conservative parties supported it, as in the west, thereby enabling the RPF to profit from their personal standing rather more than they gained from the prestige of the RPF. The southern half of France, including those areas which are most hostile to communism and most conservative, has remained indifferent or hostile to its appeal (especially the Massif Central) perhaps, at least in certain cases, because the RPF has not learned how to adapt its methods to the political habits of the south and has not been wise in its choice of candidates. These factors unquestionably contribute to its weakness.

The Moderates, including not only the candidates of the National Union of Independents, Peasants and Republicans, but also those of the dissident right-wing groups, the *pétainiste* UNIR, the Taxpayers Defense group, and the RGRIF, lost more than one-fourth of their 1946 vote. This loss can be explained by the fact that they were competing both with the RPF, which captured many of their old supporters in certain areas, and the RGR. In 1946 the RGR and the Moderates had agreed to share the constituencies on a planned basis, an operation which undoubtedly brought more Radical votes to the Moderates than it brought Moderate votes to the RGR. The election of June 17, viewed from the standpoint of voting strength, was far from the triumph of the old Right that some people had expected it would be and that some commentators have, even after the election, claimed that it was, although it is true that these people base their comments more on the number of seats won by the Moderates than on the number of votes they received.

The geographical areas in which the Moderates are strong (map 6) are highly localized, since they won over 20 per cent of the registered voters in only fifteen constituencies out of one hundred and three. These areas are principally in eastern France (Burgundy, part of Lorraine and of Franche-Comté) rather than in the west; in part of the Alps region and, especially, in the Massif Central. These are all almost exclusively rural areas, although they are not all areas where Catholicism is strong. In Burgundy, in particular, the old Right is stronger today than it was before the war in departments which are rather indifferent to religion and which are even somewhat unchristian. In these areas, the motivation of the voters is pure social conservatism, without any metaphysical ingredients.

Like the Moderates, and for the same reasons, the RGR again lost votes in 1951. Although it failed to contest seats in only fifteen departments, compared with twenty-three in 1946, the RGR lost about 7 per cent of its voters and seems definitely to have become the weakest of the major French political groups. This has caused a great deal of disappointment at the headquarters of the Radical-Socialist party, where the increase in the influence of radicalism in Parliament and its gains on the local level since 1947 had created hopes of a general increase in its strength. This did not take place, however, because the Radicals, just like the Moderates, were hit hard by the competition of the RPF, and because part of the middle classes which abandoned them in 1945 and 1946 for the MRP have remained loyal to Christian De-

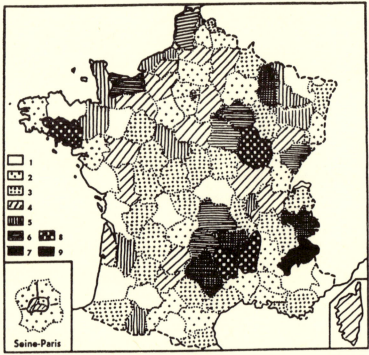

Map 6. Moderate votes (per cent of registered voters) in the National Assembly elections of June 17, 1951.

1. No votes.[1]
2. Less than 5 per cent.[2]
3. From 5 to 10 per cent.[3]
4. From 10 to 15 per cent.
5. From 15 to 20 per cent.
6. From 20 to 25 per cent.
7. From 25 to 30 per cent.
8. From 30 to 35 per cent.
9. More than 40 per cent.

[1] In Alpes-Maritimes and Côtes-du-Nord, the Moderates participated in coalition lists with Radical preponderance; in Moselle and in Vendée, they participated in, respectively, MRP and RPF-controlled lists.
[2] In Jura, participation in RGR list; in Eure-et-Loir, in RPF list.
[3] In Loire, participation in MRP list.

mocracy. In addition, the position of the Radicals as both an anticlerical and conservative party is a delicate one, as their anticlericalism seems less convincing than that of the Socialists and their conservatism less resolute than that of the genuine Moderates.

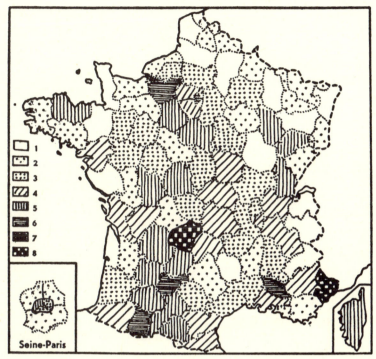

Map 7. RGR votes (per cent of registered voters) in the National
Assembly elections of June 17, 1951.

1. No votes.[1]
2. Less than 5 per cent.
3. From 5 to 10 per cent.[2]
4. From 10 to 15 per cent.

5. From 15 to 20 per cent.
6. From 20 to 25 per cent.
7. From 25 to 30 per cent.
8. From 30 to 35 per cent.

[1] In Côte-d'Or and Meuse, RGR participation in Independent list. In
Vendée, Savoie, and Haute-Savoie, in Socialist-controlled lists.
[2] In Loire, participation in MRP list.

Geographically (see map 7), radicalism is centered in the southwest, in part of central France, and to the south and the west of
the Parisian basin. It is strong also in some parts of Champagne
and Franche-Comté, as well as in some parts of the southeast.
These are essentially rural areas, sparsely populated, which have
a static economic structure and where the social climate has to a
large extent remained unchanged for half a century. The loyalty

of these areas to radicalism reflects a certain lag behind the general development of the country. In the large cities and in industrial regions, this sort of traditional radicalism is very weak, and where it still exists, as in Lyons because of the personal appeal of Edouard Herriot, it is sharply declining.

But the 1951 election revealed, in Paris, a new variety of radicalism. This new radicalism ignores the slogans of earlier days, especially that of anticlericalism, and presents itself essentially as a conservative party hostile to collectivism, in favor of "straightening out" the social reforms of the Liberation, favorably disposed towards a settlement of the religious question that will satisfy the Catholics—in short, a party appealing exclusively to right-wing voters. This sort of radicalism is hardly distinguishable from the Moderates, but it is able occasionally to steal from them the voters who think it is wise to confide the defense of their interests to a party which still retains from its past a certain aura of the Left and which therefore may not run into the same difficulties in making its views prevail as would the undisguised Right. Sometimes, as at Nice, it is the old conservatives who assume the Radical label, although this signifies absolutely no change in their conservative position.

The Popular Republicans lost half of their 1946 voters on June 17. This was a serious setback, but the net result was satisfactory. In the 1947 municipal elections the MRP had lost, in the cities, almost three-fourths of its voters of the preceding fall, and had done even worse in the countryside. It always takes a new party a long time to work its way into the municipal and departmental councils, even if it is able to win a sizable vote at a general election. The MRP, therefore, won back between 1947 and 1951 about one-third of the votes it had lost between 1946 and 1947. Its electorate remains larger than that of the Moderates or of the Radicals, something that has greatly annoyed the latter. The main point, however, is that the MRP's voters now form a much more homogeneous area of opinion than was the case in 1945 and 1946. Immediately after the Liberation, people often voted for the MRP for the lack of something better, just to make their votes count, without approving of the MRP's doctrine and program and without sharing its desire to link respect for and defense of religious values with major social reforms and the improvement of democracy. Today the strictly conservative voters, as well as those who want an authoritarian regime, have abandoned the MRP because the circumstances surrounding the election of June 17 were such that, by voting Moderate, or Radical, or RPF, one seemed to be running less of a risk of wasting a vote than by voting for the MRP. In other words, the MRP no longer profited from the premium that goes to the large parties. It is all the more remarkable that the MRP received almost two and one-half million votes. It cannot be said that its voters remained faithful only because of its position on the religious issue, for the Moderates or the RPF were as firm on that point as the MRP. It was as the representatives of Christian Democracy, in the political and in the social senses of the term, that the Popular Republicans received the support of a significant portion of the electorate, which shares to a greater degree than it did in 1945 and 1946 the preoccupations and sentiments of the leaders and the militants of the party for which it voted.

Geographically (map 8), the MRP's strongholds have shrunk considerably since 1946. The MRP remains quite strong in the west, in Alsace, in Moselle, and in some isolated departments like Jura, Haute-Savoie, Loire, and Basses-Pyrénées. (In the last two departments it had formed coalition lists.) Most, but not all, of these departments are areas where Catholicism is strong. In departments like Jura or Drôme, however, this is not the case. The MRP is still undoubtedly able to win votes from non-Catholics. Nevertheless, it tends to appear more distinctly than it did in 1945 and 1946 to be a religious party. Moreover, although it is stronger than its predecessor, the Popular Democratic Party, was during the Third Republic, and although its strength is more widespread, the MRP is a party which is really strong only in certain limited regions of the country.

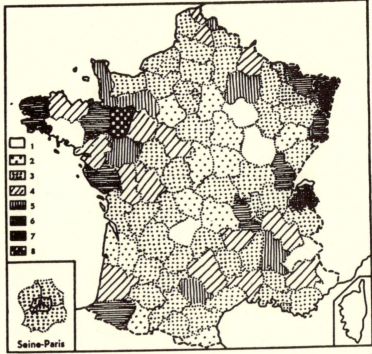

Map 8. MRP votes (per cent of registered voters) in the National Assembly elections of June 17, 1951.

1. No votes.[1]
2. Less than 5 per cent.
3. From 5 to 10 per cent.
4. From 10 to 15 per cent.
5. From 15 to 20 per cent.
6. From 20 to 25 per cent.
7. From 25 to 30 per cent.
8. From 30 to 35 per cent.

[1] In Hautes-Alpes, Côte-d'Or, and Morbihan, the MRP participated in an Independent coalition. In Corrèze, in a Radical-controlled list.

The Socialist party suffered another setback on June 17. It lost 650,000 voters, or almost 19 per cent of its 1946 electorate. It has lost more than 1,750,000 votes since October 21, 1945, more than 38 per cent of its total vote at that time. The persistence of this decline is significant. Socialism has lost voters both to the Left and to the Right. It has lost them to the Left because it broke with the Communists and renounced the tradition of working-class unity. It has lost them to the Right because it has never dared frankly and without reluctance to collaborate with the other Center parties. This policy has left it to bear the responsibility for the instability of the governments of the enlarged Third Force. The position of a party which is too anxious to defend the interests of the proletariat to be able to accept permanent compromises with the parties which are pressured by business interests and the middle classes is obviously a difficult one. It seems, however, that the French Socialist party has been particularly lacking in political imagination. It has not been able to, or has not wanted to, revitalize the doctrine that it inherited from its founders at the beginning of the twentieth century and which hardly bears any relation to the problems of today. Its decadence is to a certain extent the consequence of its excessive attachment to an obsolete orthodoxy.

The map of the Socialist vote (map 9) testifies to its weakness. The Socialist party is the only one of the major French parties which did not win the votes of one-fourth of the registered voters in a single electoral district. It is true that where the RGR captured more than 25 per cent of the registered voters, in Corrèze and in Alpes-Maritimes, it was because it had formed coalition lists. But even where the Socialists formed coalition lists, in Savoie, in Haute-Savoie, and in Vendée, they were far from successful. On the other hand, the distribution of the Socialist voters is quite uniform; the Socialist party won less than 5 per cent of the registered voters in fewer constituencies than did the MRP.

The main bastions of socialism are today in the rural departments of southern France. But the Socialist party is also still strong in certain working-class districts, in Nord, Pas-de-Calais, and Haute-Vienne in particular. Its geographical and social basis is diversified, and the lack of sociological homogeneity of its electorate contributes toward preventing it from making a choice between maintaining its character as a revolutionary party of the working class and becoming a sort of reform party, something like the old Radical-Socialist party. Actually, there can be no doubt

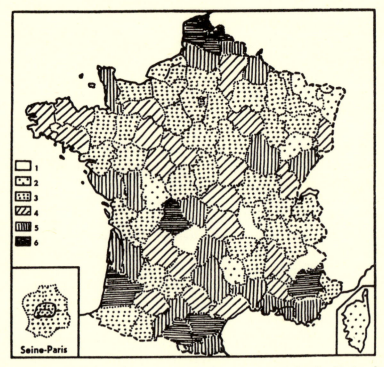

Map 9. Socialist votes (per cent of registered voters) in the National Assembly elections of June 17, 1951.

1. No votes.[1]
2. Less than 5 per cent.
3. From 5 to 10 per cent.

4. From 10 to 15 per cent.
5. From 15 to 20 per cent.
6. From 20 to 25 per cent.

[1] In Corrèze and Loire, the Socialists participated in a Radical-controlled list. In Hautes-Alpes they supported an Independent-MRP coalition list.

that it is now becoming just such a reform party by an evolutionary process that is probably irreversible. But it dares not acknowledge this openly and act accordingly and thus constantly weakens its position.

The preceding analysis of the individual parties must be completed by an analysis of the groups of parties which were formed by the alliances. For purposes of simplification, four main groups can be distinguished. First, there is the RPF opposition, to which can be added the votes that went to the parties with which the RPF agreed to ally itself in some departments. Then there is the extreme Left opposition, composed exclusively of parties which were not allied: the Communist party; the International Communist party (Trotskyite); the French Communist Movement (a "Titoist" movement launched without notable success before the election by M. Darius Le Corre, a former Communist deputy from Seine-et-Oise); the United Socialist party (a small group of dissident Socialists composed of advocates of collaboration with the Communists); and, especially, the Neutralists.

The Center parties can be divided into two groups. First, there is the Right Center, consisting on the one hand of the alliances excluding the Socialists and, on the other hand, of the Moderates and the Radicals separately. Then, there is a coalition of the Right Center and the Left Center, composed on the one hand of four-way alliances among the Moderates, Radicals, Socialists, and Popular Republicans, and on the other hand of the Socialists, Popular Republicans and Radicals separately. Maps 10, 11, 12, and 13 [5] have been drawn on the basis of this classification.

A comparison of these four maps clearly demonstrates that the coalition of the Left Center and the Right Center surpasses each of the three other groups by far in popular support. But it also demonstrates that in northern and eastern France, this political tendency, which forms the core of the majority produced by the election of June 17, is clearly in the minority. The departments of these regions are the most highly developed industrially and the ones which have a large proletariat. It is in these departments that the essential problems of our times—housing, the relationship between prices and wages, productivity—are most acute. It is these departments which create France's wealth, measured in modern terms and not according to the criteria of the nineteenth century,

---

[5] These maps are based on percentage spreads of 7.5 points, while the preceding ones, which involve smaller numbers of votes, were based on spreads of 5 points. They cannot directly be compared with one another.

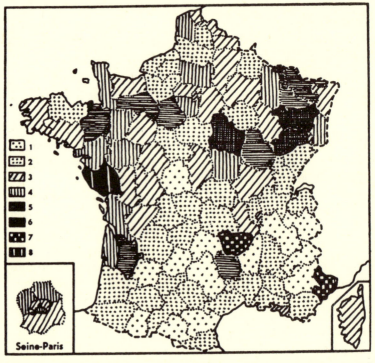

Map 10. Combined votes of RPF and RPF-allied lists (per cent of registered voters) in the National Assembly elections of June 17, 1951.

1. Less than 7.5 per cent.
2. From 7.5 to 15 per cent.
3. From 15 to 22.5 per cent.
4. From 22.5 to 30 per cent.

5. From 30 to 37.5 per cent.
6. From 37.5 to 45 per cent.
7. From 45 to 52.5 per cent.
8. From 52.5 to 60 per cent.

when family farms and small workshops were more important than great industries. One cannot fail to observe that the center of political gravity in France, located by the election of 1951 in the agricultural areas of the southwest, the southeast, and central France, coincides in no way with its center of economic gravity, which is in the north and the northeast.

A detailed statistical study of the results of the election of June

17 confirms this statement. In the seventeen departments [6] where the industrial proletariat, that is, the wage earners of enterprises employing more than ten persons in basic industries, manufacturing, transportation and public utilities, constituted more than 20 per cent of the active population in 1936, the distribution of the popular vote was very different from what it was in the rest of France, as table 2 indicates.

Table 2. Distribution of popular vote according to industrialization.

	17 Industrial Depts.		73 Other Depts.	
	Votes	%	*Votes*	%
Registered Voters	8,808,904	100	15,712,997	100
Abstentions	1,558,165	17.6	3,303,201	21.2
Communist party	1,985,682	22.4	2,948,700	18.8
RPF	1,752,889	19.8	2,512,916	15.9
Moderates	686,151	7.8	1,609,055	10.2
RGR	439,312	4.9	1,540,934	9.8
MRP	988,206	11.2	1,465,626	9.3
Socialist party	1,002,321	11.4	1,781,384	11.3
Miscellaneous	151,638	1.7	87,725	0.5

The two opposition parties, the RPF and the Communist party, received together the votes of 42.2 per cent of the registered voters in the seventeen industrial departments, compared with 35.3 per cent received by the Center parties. In the rest of France, the opposition won the votes of only 34.7 per cent of the registered voters, compared with 40.6 per cent won by the government parties. In other words, the parties of the Center have a majority in the country as a whole because of the votes they received in those parts of France which are least dynamic economically and least modernized.

The two opposition parties are stronger in industrial France

[6] Ardennes, Aube, Belfort, Bouches-du-Rhône, Doubs, Isère, Loire, Meurthe-et-Moselle, Moselle, Nord, Oise, Pas-de-Calais, Bas-Rhin, Haut-Rhin, Rhône, Seine, Somme.

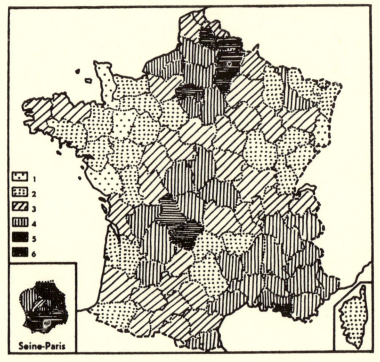

Map 11. Votes of the Extreme Left (per cent of registered voters) in the National Assembly elections of June 17, 1951.

1. Less than 7.5 per cent.
2. From 7.5 to 15 per cent.
3. From 15 to 22.5 per cent.
4. From 22.5 to 30 per cent.
5. From 30 to 37.5 per cent.
6. From 37.5 to 45 per cent.

than in the other regions by almost the same margin: the gap between the percentage of votes received by the RPF in the two types of areas is 3.9, and for the Communist party 3.6. The MRP is next, with greater strength in industrial France by a margin of 2.9. The Socialists have almost exactly the same percentage of votes in each of the two categories of departments, which confirms what has been remarked above about the sociological diversity of their electoral support and about the fundamental ambiguity in their political position which results from it. The

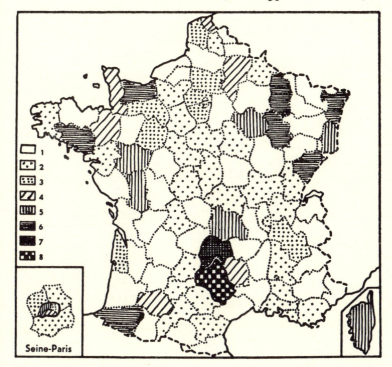

Map 12. Votes of the Right Center (per cent of registered voters) in the
National Assembly elections of June 17, 1951.

1. No votes.
2. Less than 7.5 per cent.
3. From 7.5 to 15 per cent.
4. From 15 to 22.5 per cent.

5. From 22.5 to 30 per cent.
6. From 30 to 37.5 per cent.
7. From 37.5 to 45 per cent.
8. From 45 to 52.5 per cent.

Moderates and Radicals are, on the other hand, distinctly weaker
in industrial France than they are in the less dynamic regions. The
gap is 2.4 for the Moderates and 4.9 for the RGR, and the percentile vote received by the latter in industrial France is precisely
one-half its percentile strength in the less industrial areas.

Identical conclusions are reached if the departments are classi-
fied, not according to the percentage of the population in industrial activity of a certain kind, but according to the general index

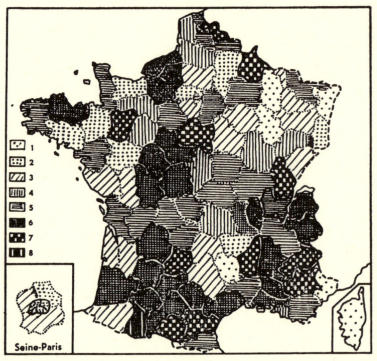

Map 13. Combined votes of the Right Center and Left Center (per cent of registered voters) in the National Assembly elections of June 17, 1951.

1. Less than 7.5 per cent.
2. From 7.5 to 15 per cent.
3. From 15 to 22.5 per cent.
4. From 22.5 to 30 per cent.

5. From 30 to 37.5 per cent.
6. From 37.5 to 45 per cent.
7. From 45 to 52.5 per cent.
8. From 52.5 to 60 per cent.

of productivity calculated by the National Institute of Statistics and Economic Studies on the basis of agricultural, commercial, craft, and industrial activity. This index is above the national average of one hundred in twenty-six departments [7] and below it

[7] Aisne, Ardennes, Aude, Belfort, Bouches-du-Rhône, Eure-et-Loire, Gard, Gironde, Hérault, Loire, Marne, Meurthe-et-Moselle, Meuse, Moselle, Nord, Oise, Pas-de-Calais, Pyrénées-Orientales, Bas-Rhin, Haut-Rhin, Rhône, Seine, Seine-Inférieure, Seine-et-Marne, Somme, Vaucluse.

in sixty-four departments. The distribution of the various parties'
votes in the two categories of departments is shown in table 3.

Table 3. Distribution of popular vote according to productivity.

	26 Highly Productive Departments		64 Less Productive Departments	
	Votes	%	*Votes*	%
Registered Voters	11,136,730	100	13,385,171	100
Abstentions	2,014,556	18	2,846,810	21.2
Communist party	2,497,675	22.4	2,436,707	18.2
RPF	2,158,609	19.3	2,107,196	15.7
Moderates	880,840	7.9	1,414,366	10.5
RGR	610,938	5.4	1,369,308	10.2
MRP	1,152,775	10.3	1,301,057	9.7
Socialist party	1,316,267	11.8	1,467,438	10.9
Miscellaneous	179,103	1.6	60,260	0.4

The differences in the percentage vote received by each party in
each of the categories of departments is about the same as revealed
by table 2, and the conclusions that have been drawn from them,
which will be discussed later in terms of their basic significance,
are confirmed.

The Strength of the Parties in the Assembly

Even under the system established by the electoral law of 1946,
the representation produced was only roughly proportional because of the small size of a great many electoral districts and because of the advantages which the distribution of seats according
to the highest average gives to the larger parties. The system established by the law of May 9, 1951, which embodied in part the
majority principle, prevented any close relationship between the
number of votes received by a party and the number of deputies
elected from that party. After having analyzed the strength of the
different political groups in the country at large, it is therefore
necessary to discuss the composition of the National Assembly.

The main objective of the authors of the law of May 9, 1951, had been to reduce the parliamentary representation of the Communist party. This goal was all the more effectively attained because the number of votes received by the Communists declined by 9 per cent. But the reduction in the number of Communist deputies was much more striking since, if the four crypto-Communists who call themselves Progressive Republicans are included, the Communist group now has 101 deputies compared with 189 in the first legislature. Assuming that the distribution of votes would have been the same even with another electoral law, it has been calculated [8] that the application of the 1946 electoral law would have given the Communists 180 seats, and the application of a system of proportional representation based on the largest remainder would have given them 159 seats. Under the 1951 law, the Communists would have won at least twenty-two fewer seats if the Center parties had formed everywhere a general alliance including the Moderates, RGR, Popular Republicans, and Socialists.

The RPF was very weak in the Assembly that had been elected in 1946 since the group of "pure Gaullists," the Group for Democratic and Social Action, had only twenty-four members, who had mostly been elected as Popular Republicans or as members of the UDSR. There was no possibility that the law of 1951 would prevent the RPF's parliamentary strength from increasing sharply, and, in fact, the RPF holds 120 seats in the new Assembly. But the authors of the 1951 law hoped that it would hold the RPF somewhat in check, and on this point they were satisfied. The 1946 law would have given the RPF 144 seats; proportional representation based on the largest remainder would have given them 133. In contrast, if the Center parties had been united everywhere, the RPF would have won only seventy-three seats in 1951.

These figures show that the maintenance of the 1946 law would have given an absolute majority in the Assembly (180 + 144 = 324 seats) to the two parties of the opposition. Proportional representa-

[8] Peter Campbell, "Remarques sur les effets de la loi electorale française du 9 mai 1951," *Revue Française de Science Politique,* October–December 1951.

tion based on the largest remainder would have given an absolute majority in the new Assembly to the Center parties, because of their slight majority of votes in the country at large, although their parliamentary majority would have been considerably smaller than it is now because of the advantages that the majority principle gave to coalitions of allied parties.

The Moderates won about one hundred seats on June 17; the 1946 law would have given them eighty; and proportional representation based on the largest remainder would have given them about eighty-five. The conclusion of quadripartite alliances in every district, however, would have given them almost 120 seats.

The RGR has ninety seats; the law of 1946 would have given it only sixty; proportional representation based on the largest remainder would have given it sixty-five. Quadripartite alliances everywhere would have boosted its total to over one hundred seats.

The MRP has eighty-seven deputies, to whom must be added the ten Overseas Independents, who have decided to attach themselves to the MRP group in the Assembly. The 1946 law would have given the MRP only about sixty seats; proportional representation based on the largest remainder would have given them about seventy-five. If quadripartite alliances had been made everywhere, the MRP would have gained an additional sixteen seats.

The Socialists, who won 107 seats on June 17, would have been reduced to eighty-six seats by the law of 1946 and to ninety-three seats by proportional representation based on the largest remainder. They would have received 131 seats if Center alliances had been made in every department.

There are also about ten deputies in the Assembly who belong to no particular group. Most of these independent deputies are representatives of the overseas territories of the French Union, and they often vote as do the Overseas Independents who are attached to the MRP group.

Everything considered, the composition of the National Assembly elected on June 17 verifies the prediction made before the election by Premier Henri Queuille: there is a "hexagonal" Assembly in which each of the six main political groups has about one hundred representatives, a few more than one hundred for the RPF and the Socialists and a few less than one hundred for the RGR and the MRP.

Were the electoral coalition of the four Center groups to succeed in maintaining its cohesiveness, the Assembly could produce a strong governing majority, opposed by two parties large enough to make their voices heard and to check the majority but weak enough to be unable to make their views prevail. There would therefore exist the necessary conditions for the proper operation of the parliamentary system. In order to accomplish that, however, the four parties of the majority would have to have a common governmental program. It has already been pointed out that the major defect of the electoral law of May 9, 1951 is that it did nothing to compel these parties to harmonize their points of view and to come to such a compromise. The electoral law created among them a solidarity that was purely negative, based only on their common, but temporary, electoral interest in defeating both the Gaullists and the Communists. Immediately after the election, there were good reasons for fearing that the new Assembly would be able to produce a real governing majority only with great difficulty. This fear was substantiated quickly, during the debates of the first session which opened on July 5 and continued until September 25, 1951.

IV

Party Conflicts in the
New National Assembly

It is hardly necessary to restate the issues on which the Center parties disagreed with one another, although their common hostility to the RPF and the Communists had led them to make common cause for the election of June 17. It has been pointed out in Chapter I that the Socialists and many of the Popular Republicans did not accept without protest the liberal economic policy advocated by the RGR and the Moderates, and at least partially imposed by them on the governments of the enlarged Third Force, since that policy was more solicitous of the interests of management than of those of wage earners. On several occasions, but always in vain, the Socialists had provoked ministerial crises in order to try to make their opinions prevail. They had even withdrawn from the cabinet entirely from February to July of 1950. Although they had returned to the Pleven cabinet after the out-break of the Korean war, the idea of returning to the opposition was very tempting to the Socialists after the June election, as they felt that their working-class electoral clientele had taken them to task because of their collaboration in the government with the conservative parties.

The Areas of Discord among the Center Parties

From 1947 to 1951, the Socialists and the Popular Republicans constituted the largest fraction of the Center majority. They had had to make serious concessions to the RGR and to the Moderates, and bore a special responsibility because of their numbers. After the June election, the greatly increased importance of the liberal elements of the Center seemed to transfer this responsibility to them. The Socialists felt that it was now up to their partners to come, cap in hand, to ask for support on their Left. This the Socialists would give them at the stiffest possible price in terms of measures designed to help the wage earners. A good many Popular Republicans shared this attitude.

The Moderates and the Radicals, however, who had gained in the Assembly (although they had lost votes in the country since 1946), claimed that the results of the June election had condemned *dirigisme* and all socialistically inclined measures. Although it was really doubtful that the RPF agreed with them on economic, social, and financial policy, in one sense its activities had provided some reason for believing that its 120 deputies could be added to the one hundred Moderates and the ninety members of the RGR to form a liberal bloc that would have almost an absolute majority in the Assembly and which would in any case dominate the noncommunist area of the Assembly. The grounds for such reasoning had been provided by the RPF's criticism of the Center governments, criticism that was often made thoughtlessly and which was designed simply to make its propaganda as effective as possible. In any event, the Peasants, the Independents, and the Radicals were in no way inclined to make concessions to socialism. Quite the contrary, they reasoned that it was necessary to decide squarely in favor of a liberal economic policy. The result was that, right after its electoral victory of June 17, the Center majority was more deeply divided over economic matters than it had been during the preceding National Assembly.

Another divisive element, which had lain dormant for a long time, appeared to complicate the situation further: the question of the church schools. The MRP and the Moderates had not been successful in 1948 in preventing the secularization of the schools belonging to the nationalized coal mines or in securing financial aid for private schools through the medium of public grants to parents' associations, which the Poinso-Chapuis decree would have permitted. But they had not accepted their defeat as final and had always expressly reserved the right to raise the question again when circumstances seemed more favorable. A certain amount of agitation had occurred in western France over this question in 1950. Some of the parents of children who attended church schools, dissatisfied because they paid taxes to support secular schools to which they did not wish to send their children, had been encouraged by some of the Catholic clergy to go on a tax strike. The MRP had contributed greatly to successful negotiations which were carried out with the Vatican, after which the latter had advised the French church hierarchy to put an end to the tax strike. But the Popular Republicans were completely resolved to persist in their efforts to secure financial help for the private schools, as their promise to do so had played a large role in the success of the 'negotiations with the Holy See over the tax strike. Moreover, the RPF, which had taken a position in favor of revising the school legislation inherited from Jules Ferry, was trying to conquer the MRP's Catholic voters by claiming that the MRP was ready to sacrifice the private schools to their political alliance with the Socialists.

In June and July of 1950, at the time of the investiture of Henri Queuille and then of René Pleven, the MRP's spokesmen demanded as a condition for their support the initiation of studies to revise the school legislation. Pleven promised to establish a committee of experts, including mainly representatives of public and private education, who would be charged with examining all the aspects of the problem. This committee was formed at the beginning of the fall of 1950, under the chairmanship of J. Paul-Boncour, a former Premier and a member of the Socialist party, a broadminded man now retired from active political life.

The French Catholics had always affirmed the legitimacy of contributing public funds for private education, but the question had taken on special urgency since the Liberation. From 1941 to 1944, the Vichy regime had given substantial aid to the private schools, and the cessation of this aid at the end of the school year of 1944–1945 had created difficult problems for these schools. The social groups which had formerly borne the major expenses of Catholic education, the old *bourgeoisie* and landed nobility, had become considerably poorer since 1914, and the resources that they put at the disposal of the Church for its schools no longer matched its needs. In addition, the salaries of teachers in private schools were ridiculously low.

French public opinion had also become impressed, under the influence of socialist ideas, with the notion that strictly juridical and formal liberty is fallacious unless there is an economic basis which permits liberty to be realized in practice. It was this principle which instigated the reforms carried out in the social sphere between the two wars. The principle of freedom of education, in the double sense of the freedom for every competent person to open a school and for the head of the family to send his children to the school of his choice—a principle inherited from the Third Republic—was accepted by the majority of the country, including the Radicals and a number of Socialists. The Catholics considered themselves justified in demanding that this theoretical liberty be made effective by appropriate financial measures, that is, by governmental subsidies which would permit the private schools to pay their teachers decent salaries and not require financial sacrifices by the parents of their pupils.

The sharp rise in the birth rate since 1945 has caused an increase in the number of children of school age which is bound to grow even larger during the coming years, and the public schools will not be able, for lack of teachers and school facilities, to provide education for all the children. In fact, there could be compulsory education only because of the existence of the private schools. The Catholics reason that, as they participate in performing a public service, they should be aided by the state.

The question of the survival of private schools is of vital importance to the French Catholic Church because priests are recruited almost exclusively among the former students of private schools. The proportion of priests who were students in the public schools hardly exceeds 30 per cent where this proportion is greatest —i.e., in the Paris area, as well as the dioceses of Bordeaux, Marseilles, Avignon, Valence and Besançon—although there is a slight tendency for this proportion to increase.[1]

The claims of the Church in educational matters, however, clash with the strong hostility of left-wing opinion. This hostility can be explained, first of all, by history. During the first years of the Third Republic, at the time when there was still a deep solidarity between the Church and the monarchist parties, the secularization of public primary education, accomplished by Jules Ferry, symbolized the victory of the republicans at the same time that it consolidated this victory by withdrawing the training of future citizens from the influence of the Church. The principle that no aid coming from public funds, whether those of the central government, the departments, or the towns, would be granted to the private primary schools was embodied in a law of 1886. This principle quickly took on a veritably sacrosanct character for the parties of the Left. For a long time the dogma of the incontrovertibility of the "lay laws" served as the criterion for distinguishing republicans from reactionaries and enabled the former to unite in at least one domain even while they differed in all the others. The fact that the Vichy government had granted subsidies to the private schools naturally enhanced even further the symbolic significance of the old legislation which Vichy had abrogated and which was restored in 1945.

[1] Chanoine Boulard, *Essor ou declin du clergé français* (Paris, 1950), pp.137, 154.

The Radical-Socialist party, for a long time the leader of the anticlerical chorus, had somewhat relaxed its stubbornness on this question since the political situation had led it to solicit the votes of a rather conservative portion of the population. While it accepted freedom of education (which some of its leaders had fought at the beginning of the twentieth century), it opposed overturning the school legislation of Jules Ferry, for it realized that its attachment to the old conception of secularism was the only mark that distinguished it from the Moderates.

The Socialist party, originally less dogmatic on religious questions than the Radicals, had progressively stiffened its position as the old Radical voters, especially the public-school teachers, joined its ranks and as its center of electoral support shifted into the rural departments of the Midi, where a part of the population is not merely indifferent but definitely hostile to religion.

The Communist party has two reasons for opposing the private schools. The first and undoubtedly the more important one is that it is well aware that the influence of the Catholic Church and of religious ideas generally constitutes one of the principal obstacles impeding the complete conquest of mind and heart which it is bent on accomplishing. The second reason is a tactical one; in posing as the champion of secularism, it attaches itself to the tradition of the left-wing parties of the nineteenth and the early twentieth centuries. This is the principal factor in its success in many of the rural departments of central and southern France. In addition, this tactic provides an effective way of dividing its adversaries, in particular the Socialists and the Popular Republicans.

In order to complete this survey of the religious problem, it is necessary to point out that it varies in importance in different parts of France. Of the 5,132,786 children who received primary education in 1949–1950, only 910,064, less than 18 per cent of the total, were students in private schools. But they were not distributed uniformly over France, as is illustrated by map 14. There are two regions where the percentage of students attend-

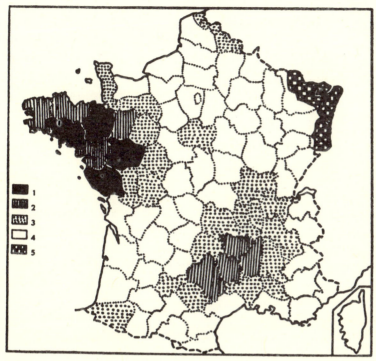

Map 14. Attendance at private primary schools (per cent of children of school age) during the 1949–50 school year.

1. More than 50 per cent.   3. From 15 to 30 per cent.
2. From 30 to 50 per cent.   4. Less than 15 per cent.
    5. Departments of Alsace and Lorraine, where the public school system is not governed by the lay principles that apply to the rest of France.

ing private schools is large, the west and the southern part of the Massif Central. In addition, there are the three departments of Alsace and Lorraine recovered from Germany in 1919; there the secular school legislation, which was enacted while they were annexed to Germany, has never been put into effect. These departments are still under the Falloux law of 1850 which guarantees that public education shall have religious content and, of course, the problem of subsidies to private schools does not exist there,

since the public schools, which are supported by the central government and the towns, are organized and staffed in a way that is
satisfactory to the Catholics. But there is no doubt that the great
majority of the population of this area would not accept the
secularization of the school system.

For the rest of France, the map showing the distribution of the
students attending private schools is not identical with that in-
dicating the degrees of religious intensity.[2] There are Catholic departments in Lorraine, in Franche-Comté, and in Savoie where
less than 15 per cent of the children attend private schools. This
is a revealing indication of the different psychological attitudes
of Catholic families toward the public schools. Except in a dozen
departments in the west and in the Massif Central, the public
schools no longer arouse the fears and the suspicion that were
current fifty or sixty years ago. The education given in the public
schools is nonreligious, but not antireligious, and it does not appear to the parents or even to the clergy to be a threat to the beliefs
of the children.

The situation is different where the private schools have a great
many students. There, the public schools, born in a belligerent
atmosphere, assume an unquestionably aggressive, secular character. This only serves, naturally, to perpetuate the discord and
sharpen the mutual resentment between the partisans of the
"Christian school" and of the "Godless school."

Politically, the chronic dissatisfaction of the Catholic inhabitants of the west and of the southern part of the Massif Central,
although it could be annoying, was not of decisive importance as
long as their deputies belonged to the antirepublican opposition
or, even after they had rallied to the Republic, as long as their support was not necessary for the formation of governing majorities.
Since 1945, however, the strengthening of communism in other
parts of the country has reversed this situation. The Center majority which governed from 1947 to 1951 would not have been
able to exist without the support of many deputies from areas

[2] *Ibid.,* p. 169.

where the private schools have the confidence of a majority or of a very large proportion of the families. It was inevitable, under these circumstances, that the question of changing the school legislation would be raised as soon as circumstances gave the defenders of the private schools a real opportunity to make their views prevail.

This opportunity appeared after the 1951 election. The Communist voters were underrepresented in Parliament because of the effects of the electoral law and of the isolation of the Communist party; the consequence was that a majority of the deputies elected were in favor of aid to the private schools, although it is not certain that this parliamentary majority rests on a corresponding majority in the country. The division of the advocates of subsidies to private schools between the RPF and the Center coalition made it inevitable that the question would quickly be raised before the National Assembly. Each of the two groups was afraid that the other would try to attract its voters by taking the initiative in changing the secular school laws. The fear of each group that it would be outbid by the other caused the school question to be raised in Parliament before the Paul-Boncour committee had arrived at its conclusions. Furthermore, the fact that the Socialists wanted to break with their liberal partners in the Center coalition over economic policy made it certain, in advance, that they would be uncompromising in their defense of the traditional conception of secularism, because that would enable them to shift to their former allies the responsibility for the dislocation of the majority.

The Difficulties in Electing a Premier

The Catholic leaders of the movement for revising the educational laws created a Parliamentary Association for Educational Liberty, the understanding being that its members would consult with one another and adopt a common position in order to prevent the political divisions among the advocates of subsidies for private schools from leading them to try to outbid one another, something which might eventually play into the hands of the anticlericals who wanted to maintain the *status quo*. Several days after the opening of the Assembly, however, on July 5, the RPF group introduced a bill to establish educational grants in conformity with the program adopted by its national congress at Lille in 1949. Grants would be given to all parents of children attending primary schools, whether public or private, and would enable those parents whose children did not receive the free education provided by the state schools to contribute to the support of the schools they preferred. This move, which seemed contrary to the agreement made by the members of the Parliamentary Association to act in concert, strengthened the determination of the Moderates and the Popular Republicans to demand at once the passage of a law favoring private schools. They could not afford to wait until the Paul-Boncour committee presented its recommendations, which were expected in the fall (if the doubtful assumption was made that the members of the committee could arrive at an agreement satisfactory to all). Because the partial election of departmental councilors was scheduled for October, the Center parties would by delaying action on the school question be furnishing their Gaullist adversaries with a damaging issue.

There was another consideration. During the first negotiations on the new cabinet (the Queuille cabinet had to resign according to the terms of the constitution, and Queuille, pleading bad health, had refused to try to form a new government), the Moderates and the Popular Republicans agreed to demand that the future Premier promise not to oppose any proposals initiated by Parliament for the purpose of giving provisional aid to the private schools, pending the Paul-Boncour committee report. They hoped that this would make it possible for the proclerical majority in the Assembly to settle the school question without dislocating the other majority needed to govern the country. But the Socialists, and some Radicals, made their support of any Center government conditional upon that government's defending secularism —if necessary, by making it an issue of confidence. It very quickly became apparent that there was going to be an impasse.

On July 24, the Radical leader, René Mayer, who had been designated as Premier by President Auriol, tried to win the support of the National Assembly. In the fall of 1949, after the resignation of the Queuille cabinet, Mayer had had to give up trying to form a government, although he had been invested by the Assembly, because the Socialists had refused to approve his price and wage policy. It was undoubtedly his memory of this occasion which led Mayer, in his declaration of July 24, 1951, and in the debate which followed it, to preoccupy himself especially with removing any possible hostility on the part of the Socialists. With respect to the school problem, he promised, on one hand, to extend the scholarship benefits granted by the state to students of private secondary schools and, on the other hand, to establish for children of school age, whether or not they attended private schools, a supplementary family grant paid directly to their parents. These measures were acceptable to the anticlericals, because they had always been less sensitive about technical education and higher education than about primary education. Also, Mayer's second proposal did not involve direct aid to the private schools; it only enabled them to charge the parents of their pupils higher fees.

But the Catholics could not accept such limited measures. They demanded that the state aid be given not to the parents, but, if not to the schools themselves, at least to the parents' associations, because they did not want to accentuate the inequality between the public schools, where education is free, and the private schools, required by Mayer's proposals to establish relatively high fees. The MRP vainly asked Mayer to let the problem of aid to private primary schools be settled by a majority in Parliament without any intervention by the cabinet. In the end, Mayer received only 241 votes (Socialists, RGR, a small minority of the MRP and of the Moderates). He was opposed by 101 deputies (the Communists). The RPF and most of the Moderates and Popular Republicans abstained. As the Premier can be formerly invested, according to the provisions of the constitution, only by an absolute majority of the members of the National Assembly (313 votes), Mayer had to abandon his attempt to form a government.

After new negotiations, President Auriol named Maurice Petsche as Premier. The former Minister of Finance was a Moderate, but a Protestant, and one of the few members of his group who did not join the parliamentary association of defenders of private education. He presented the school problem as a matter of social justice and proposed the establishment of a special fund, to be financed through taxation, from which supplementary wages would be paid to all workers whose remuneration was below the guaranteed minimum interprofessional wage. This would provide a way to increase the salaries of the teachers in the private schools. But the principle could also be applied to many other wage earners, and it had the disadvantage of encouraging employers not to pay their employees adequate wages. Petsche was supported by the Moderates, the MRP, and the RGR. But the Socialists and the RPF abstained, and the Communists voted against him. He received only 281 votes and therefore was not invested formally as Premier.

These two successive attempts to invest a Premier, both of which failed because of the school problem, made the Center parties aware of the dangers that would arise if the majority revealed itself any longer to be incapable of creating a government. The third candidate for the post of Premier, René Pleven, was invested on August 8 by 391 votes to 102, the RPF having abstained and the Communists having opposed him. Pleven had adopted Mayer's proposal for making scholarships available to students of private secondary schools, and he announced that as far as primary education was concerned, he would not oppose any parliamentary proposals "falling within the framework" of the solutions suggested by Mayer and Petsche "and resting within their limits with respect to costs and financing."

It was only at this time that a government was finally formed, after a crisis which had lasted more than a month. The cabinet, however, was not built in the image of the majority which had invested Pleven, as the Socialists refused to participate in it. After the cabinet was formed, it succeeded on August 10 in securing from the Assembly the indefinite postponement of a debate over its composition, which was equivalent to winning a vote of confidence. Then the Socialists proposed that the parliamentary session be interrupted until October. But the majority in favor of aiding the private schools refused to accept this and decided that the Assembly would take up its work again on August 21 for a "short session" to be devoted to voting on school matters.

The Dislocation of the Center Majority Caused by the Passage of the Educational Laws

The parliamentary session started again on August 21; it had been hoped that it would last only about ten days, but actually it lasted much longer, as it was not adjourned until September 25. It was devoted almost exclusively to the discussion of two bills concerning private education, a government bill which, in conformity with the promises made by Pleven in his ministerial declaration, extended the granting of state scholarships to students attending private secondary schools, and a private member's bill introduced in the name of the Parliamentary Association for Educational Liberty by an MRP deputy, M. Barangé, and an RPF deputy, M. Barrachin.

The latter bill provided for quarterly grants of 1,000 francs each for each student attending primary school, whether public or private. In the case of the students attending public schools, the grants would go into departmental funds earmarked for the construction and improvement of public educational facilities. In the case of the students attending private schools, the grants would go to parents' associations on the condition that they use them according to the needs of the various schools. The measure was to cost more than fifteen billion francs a year, less than three billion francs of which would benefit the private schools. The necessary resources were to be obtained from a slight increase in the production tax. The bill was proposed as a provisional measure, to stand until a final reform could be enacted after the presentation of the report of the committee inquiring into the school problem. The authors hoped that the opposition of the anticlericals would be somewhat diminished because four-fifths of the funds expended would go to the public schools. But the bill took on a symbolic significance for both sides and, in addition, the opponents of the bill continually acted as though the bill would aid the private schools exclusively.

The discussion of the government bill started in the National Assembly on August 24, but it lasted a long time, as the opponents of the private schools introduced a great many substitute motions, amendments, and incidental and prejudicial motions. The bill was adopted on September 4 by 361 votes to 236. It was opposed by the Communists, the Socialists, and a small fraction of the RGR.

The Assembly began discussing the Barangé bill on the same day. The debate on this bill did not last quite as long as the preceding one, as the deputies were growing somewhat weary. The government succeeded in removing from the bill an article which would have permitted the departmental councils to subsidize associations of parents of pupils attending private schools, something that would have had the great disadvantage of perpetuating local quarrels between Catholics and anticlericals. The ministers abstained from voting on the bill, over which they disagreed. Most of the Radical ministers, however, voted in favor of a motion to adjourn the debate, which was opposed by the Moderate and Popular Republican ministers. This contributed to undermining the fiction of governmental solidarity. On September 10 the bill was finally passed by 313 votes to 255. Half the RGR joined the Socialists and the Communists in opposing it, but about ten Radicals voted for it, along with the RPF, the Moderates, and the MRP.

Contrary to certain predictions, the RPF did not try to outdo the proposals of the parliamentary association in favor of aiding private schools. Quite the contrary, all during the debates, the Gaullist spokesman tried to demonstrate that the educational grants did not contradict the fundamental principle of the separation of church and state, to which they declared their loyal attachment. It was obvious that they did not want to antagonize the left-wing followers of the RPF or to allow themselves to be identified during the debate with the old Right and the pro-clericals.

The Socialists vigorously expressed their hostility to the measure and declared that the majority had definitely been destroyed. The MRP, on the contrary, considered that the whole affair was just an episode and that once the problem was settled there would be nothing to stand in the way of its reaffirming its solidarity with the Socialists on economic matters. The MRP gave concrete evidence of its intentions during the week when the Council of the Republic was studying the school bills passed by the Assembly. The Socialists had introduced a bill establishing a sliding wage scale. The Moderates and the Radicals were very much opposed to this bill. The Popular Republicans, however, came out in favor of it, despite the objections of the government. In order to put the cabinet in a difficult position, the RPF deputies, although they stated that they opposed the bill, decided to vote for it. But Pleven sidestepped the difficulty by not posing a question of confidence and by announcing that the government, counting on the Council of the Republic to amend the bill so that it would become acceptable, would only intervene during the second reading of the bill in the Assembly. The bill was passed on September 20 by 402 votes to 191, but the Council of the Republic decided not to discuss it immediately.

The Council of the Republic had passed the school bills with some amendments, all of which, save one, were of minor importance. It opposed the method of financing the school grants proposed by the Assembly; it wanted the money to be secured through economy measures rather than by taxes. The National Assembly, however, repassed the bill in its original form, and its decision was final.

The divisions within the majority were then highlighted when the National Assembly was unable to decide on adjourning the session. Each successive proposal was rejected. The RPF wanted to hold a debate on foreign policy; the Socialists wanted the session to be continued because its adjournment would postpone the deadline for action by the Council of the Republic on the sliding wage scale bill; the Communists joined the Gaullists and the Socialists in forming a purely negative majority which might have prevented the Assembly from adjourning. But the difficulty was overcome by a procedural expedient on September 25. Inasmuch as all the proposals of the Conference of Presidents and all the amendments to these proposals had been rejected, Edouard Herriot, the President of the National Assembly, suggested that the Assembly adjourn sine die, and let him set the date for reconvening it. The suggestion was accepted.

The parliamentary recess, which was to last until November 6, started amid a most confusing political atmosphere. The Center majority had been split by the debate over the school bills and by the enactment of the sliding wage scale, and each of the two bills had split the majority in a different way. On the first issue, the MRP and the Moderates had opposed the Radicals and the Socialists; on the second, the Moderates and the Radicals had opposed the MRP and the Socialists. It was clear that it would be very difficult to recreate in Parliament and in the government the coalition which had been formed for the June election and which had at that time won a majority of the popular vote and, even more decisively, a majority of the seats in the National Assembly.

V

The Fundamental Problems of French Political Life

Viewed in its widest perspective, the political evolution of France since the Liberation has been characterized principally by the progressive disappearance of the superficial unanimity of public opinion expressed by the provisional government of General de Gaulle and later by tripartism under conditions which are recognizable today as having been largely artificial. The consequence has been the reappearance and aggravation of partisan antagonisms.

Causes and Characteristics of the Party Struggle

The changes in French political institutions and practices since 1945 have considerably increased the role of organized parties in governmental and parliamentary activity, as well as their power over public opinion. Furthermore, the widening rifts among the more and more unyielding parties—aside from the fact that there are no longer any truly independent politicians who, like Briand, for example, used to play a conciliatory role during the Third Republic—seem to be on the point of preventing the political machinery from functioning while they lead French political life into a blind alley.

The division of public opinion into numerous segments is not a new phenomenon in France, although the existence of parties corresponding to and emphasizing each segment is somewhat new. But during the Third Republic the various political groups usually fell into two blocs, for there was generally a single line of demarcation between the groups on various questions, and this enabled parliamentary majorities to be formed. These majorities were based on coalitions, of course, but they were able to govern with a certain amount of coherence. This situation started to change during the period between wars. The left-wing majorities, which were united politically and which, in 1936, included the Communist party, were disunited on economic and financial questions. After the general elections in which the left-wing parties carried the day—and this occurred on three occasions, in 1924, 1932, and 1936—they started out by governing for about two years. Then they divided and a new majority, consisting of the most moderate of the left-wing parties, which meant the Radicals, and the old right-wing opposition took over.

Things are much more complicated today. The events of the summer of 1951 demonstrated as clearly as possible that the composition of the parliamentary majority changes with each problem before Parliament. On religious or educational questions there is a majority of the Right, in the old sense of the word, which includes the RPF, the Moderates, the MRP, and some Radicals, and a left-wing minority, including the Communists, the Socialists, and most of the RGR. But in neither camp do the various parties agree among themselves on any other question. If the issue involves political institutions, a general outlook at once somewhat hostile to personal rule and extremely hostile to what the Communists call "popular" democracy is adopted by the Center majority which emerged victorious from the elections of June 17. But the various elements of this majority, agreed on what they do not want, are far from equally agreed on what they do want. The Moderates and the Radicals want to modify the constitution of 1946, for example, by giving the Council of the Republic powers similar to those formerly enjoyed by the Senate, something which is not acceptable to the Socialists or the MRP. The question of the electoral system, especially the issue of the second ballot, creates a different alignment: the MRP and some of the Moderates favor the single ballot, while the rest of the Moderates, the Gaullists, the Radicals, and probably also the Socialists want to abandon it and to return to the traditional French system of two ballots. As to the re-establishment, under one form or another, of the practice of delegated legislation and the issuance of decree-laws, the RPF favors it in theory, but would undoubtedly oppose it if it were proposed for a ministry which the RPF did not control; the Moderates and the Radicals would accept it; the Popular Republicans and the Socialists would oppose it.

The situation is particularly complicated in the realm of economic and social policy. This is the area in which, since 1947, the Center majority has been the most vulnerable, as the position of the Socialists and many of the Popular Republicans has frequently been sharply different from that of the Radicals and the Moderates. The RPF, because it was in the opposition, and because part of its electoral support came from formerly right-wing voters, has criticised *dirigisme* and governmental tax policies in terms which have made its position seem to coincide with that of the liberals. In reality, several important aspects of its program, especially the association of capital and labor and the desire to place French rearmament on as independent a basis as possible, imply a basic difference between the RPF and the liberals in their attitudes toward the role of the state in economic life and toward *dirigisme*. The complexity of these areas of disagreement embroil and divide the cluster of non-Communist parties into fractions. These fractions are often so numerous that even on an isolated problem there is no parliamentary majority. Moreover, the situation is aggravated by the Communist tactic of supporting one or another of the fractions in order to give it a negative and temporary majority, a policy which can paralyze all parliamentary and governmental activity.

The causes of this situation are numerous and complex. Nevertheless, it would not be an exaggeration to say that they stem from the fact that in French political life the past has as great an influence, if not more influence, than the present. The causes of political dispute which operated of old—when the very principles of democracy and of the Republic were contested by the Right, when the Church was, or appeared to be, a full partner of the reactionary parties, and when politics was nourished almost exclusively by quarrels of a philosophical or metaphysical nature— continue to make their weight felt in an era when it is the extreme Left which rejects liberal democracy in the traditional Western sense of the word, when the Church, or at least many Catholics, have accepted not only political democracy but social democracy, and when the vital problems of production, exchange, the standard of living, and housing are the foundation of political interest. New causes for cleavage have appeared, but the old ones have not disappeared; that is why the lines of demarcation between the parties have become so complicated and have lost all coherence and all continuity.

But why does the past survive in contemporary political life? Certainly this tendency corresponds to the national temperament. Frenchmen automatically think of politics in historical terms. Probably the prolonged struggles which took place over the principles and the heritage of the Revolution of 1789 accentuated this characteristic trait. Throughout the nineteenth century and even during the first years of the twentieth century, there has been in France a counterrevolutionary party which attributed all the difficulties and the vicissitudes of national political life to revolutionary principles and which dreamed of a return to the past in order to erase the consequences of these errors and to begin anew the history of the last century. But the Right has not been alone in turning to the past. It is significant that even today, after eighty years, the Communists and the Socialists each year piously carry out the pilgrimage from the Mur des Fédérés, to the cemetery of Père-Lachaise, in order to commemorate the participants in the Paris Commune who were shot there by Thiers' troops in

May 1871. And the Communist propaganda machine, at the time of the constitutional referendum of May 1946, plastered the walls of France with pictures of Gambetta and of Jules Ferry and claimed, somewhat paradoxically, that these great republican and patriotic statesmen "would have voted YES" if they had been alive in 1946. The intellectualism, the penchant for coherent systems of thought, and the value attached to symbols, which characterize French political life very often to the detriment of a sense of reality and a desire for concrete accomplishments, are among the psychological causes of the burden which the past places on the present.

These explanations, however, are inadequate. The fundamental cause of the phenomenon that must be explained seems to be that socially and economically the France of earlier days, the France of small farms, small workshops, small businesses, the France of individualism, where, in the words of Robert de Jouvenel, "politics is a matter of taste, it is not the condition of man's existence," [1] this France still survives today in many areas.

Under the Second Empire, Napoleon III had accelerated the modernization of economic life, especially through the free-trade commercial treaties concluded after 1860 and through a systematic program of construction, particularly in the field of transportation facilities (railroads, roads, canals, a merchant fleet, and ports). This progress slackened during the Third Republic, and France then began to fall behind the other great powers in her economic and social development. A protectionist tariff structure, erected in 1881 for agricultural products, reinforced and extended to industrial products in 1892, and accentuated again in 1910, enabled obsolete and unproductive methods to survive. France depended less upon international trade than the other great European powers. The relative smallness of her internal market did not require her to develop techniques of mass production. Thanks to these conditions, the French economy showed little sensitivity to crises and enjoyed an unquestionable stability, but this was at

[1] Robert de Jouvenel, *La République des Camarades* (Paris, 1934), p. 4.

the expense of the expansion and modernization needed by any twentieth-century nation that wanted to maintain its position among the great powers. Broad financial activities, backed by considerable savings and colonial conquests, concealed this situation, but they could not eradicate it. In many French departments, and undoubtedly in most of them, economic life in the middle of the twentieth century differed less from that of the period of the Restoration or of the July Monarchy, than from that which had developed in the industrial regions of northern and northeastern France, or around the big cities like Paris and Lyons and the ports like Nantes, Bordeaux, and Marseilles.

For France had not been uniformly stagnant economically, and some areas experienced an economic development similar to that which other countries were undergoing. The north and the northeast became industrialized and modernized after the First World War because of the necessity of restoring the shattered region which had served as a battlefield.

It has been demonstrated in Chapter III that the strength of the various political parties in the more industrialized and productive regions differs considerably from the rest of the country. The parties of more recent origin are considerably stronger in the industrial areas, while the older groups, the traditional Radical Left and traditional conservative Right, have their main bastions in the less industrialized and less productive areas. Statistical and geographic studies reveal the sociological and political diversity of France and they also explain the diversity in the preoccupations of the political parties. No party can really afford to ignore the requirements of either modern France or old France, although each party inclines toward one or the other. The parties are compelled, therefore, in order to protect themselves, to take into consideration both the automatic, historically founded reactions of part of the electorate and the more specific and concrete claims of the other part of the electorate.

The situation, of course, is not as simple as this description tends to make it appear. There are in the old parts of France citizens who share the preoccupations and the needs of modern France, and the reverse is also true. But in general, it can hardly be doubted that the sociological and economic diversity of France and the unequal degree of modernization of its various regions are largely at the bottom of the combination of ideological problems of the past and concrete problems of the present which serves to divide the parties.

This combination of problems has produced a situation that is all the more complex because France has since 1945 been undergoing a more rapid and more extensive process of economic and social change than at any other time since the Second Empire. The plan for modernization and equipment drafted by Jean Monnet and his colleagues is designed not only to enable France to make up for the unusually prolonged economic crisis of the thirties and then that of the war, but also to inject some life into the French economy which will enable it to compensate for the disappearance of income from foreign investments by increased production at home. Since 1946, when the Monnet Plan was adopted as the long-range economic policy of the state, France has carried out an investment program that is especially heavy because it is paralleled by a program of reconstruction of the property destroyed during the war. Moreover, private investment has declined considerably because of the successive devaluations of the currency (which also provoked the transfer of considerable capital from France), and this has given to the public investment program, which is partially financed through taxation, a relative importance far greater than that of any public program in the past.

The plan for modernization concerns agriculture as well as industry. For the first time in many years, the price of wheat on the domestic French market is not considerably higher than it is on the world market. Taking into consideration the devaluation of French currency, the price of wheat has been consistently lower since 1945 than it was just before the Second World War. The French peasants have been able to weather this situation because of important changes in agricultural techniques, principally the introduction of mechanization.

The rise in the birth rate since 1945—its regular decline under the Third Republic had undoubtedly been the most important symptom of not only the human, but the economic, aging of France—reinforces the evidence that the country is going through a period of transformation, the result of which must be to counterbalance the stagnation of the previous regime.

It would have been difficult enough to persuade the French people to make such an effort before the Second World War, when international conditions would not have been particularly unfavorable for it. The efforts being made today are much more burdensome for a number of reasons. The changing relations between metropolitan France and the overseas territories—what was formerly called the Empire has now become the French Union— tend to increase the costs. Exploitation of the old colonies, even if it was not carried out with modern techniques, formerly increased the net resources of metropolitan France; but today these colonies require additional investment, the effects of which will largely benefit the native populations.

The obstacles to foreign trade and the restrictions on the international credit system reduce the amount of aid which can be secured from abroad through the customary methods of finance capitalism. The aid given by the United States happily compensates in part for this collapse of the old mechanisms of a liberal economy, but it involves political considerations which necessarily lend themselves to discussion, and its precarious nature, dependent upon annual appropriations by the United States Congress, prevents France from basing her long-range plans on it. Lastly, the rearmament effort made necessary by the Korean War has added another burden—apparently sterile from the aspect of immediate results—to the economy and it provides additional political dissension.

It is not at all astonishing that the necessary acceleration of French economic development has created serious political tensions. The increase in the number of children, who consume without producing; the rise in the rate of investment; the importation of producers' goods rather than consumers' goods; and rearmament—these things present the difficult problem of how the available wealth is to be distributed. The antagonisms between the different social categories are aggravated; each tries, by every method, to defend its own interests and to maintain its former standard of living, even at the expense of the other groups. If the cleavages between the parties do not stem solely from these antagonisms, they certainly reflect them to a large extent. The regions which are least affected by the economic and social developments currently taking place naturally tend to regard them as useless and dangerous and try to avoid supporting their cost. These people find allies in certain categories of the population of the other regions, among the privileged groups who feel strong enough to be able to defend their interests effectively in a liberal system. This is the basic significance of the coalition between part of the urban business community and the rural population which expresses itself politically in hostility to *dirigisme*.

Not only are the political differences caused by current economic and social problems added to those which derive from the traditional reflexes and resentments inherited from the past, but they also contribute to perpetuating them. Each party tries to put the old slogans at the service of the interests it is defending. This is particularly clear in the case of the Communist party, which exploits the old antagonism between the proclericals and the anticlericals or the old conception of independence and national sovereignty in behalf of a policy whose objectives are quite different. But no political group is immune from the charge of exploiting for its selfish interest the old causes of political dissension at the same time that it expresses the conflicting interests and the differences of opinion which stem from contemporary problems.

It would be completely meaningless to condemn the parties which act this way. Democracy assumes the existence of tensions among different areas of opinion. It is important, however, to understand that the dissensions which make the French political situation so confusing have their roots in specific historical and social circumstances and are not simply the reflection of a sort of congenital French incapacity to adopt reasonable and effective political conduct. It is especially important, in order to understand what the fundamental political problems of France actually are, to investigate why the state for too many years has seemed to be so completely powerless to hold the antagonisms and the divisions between the parties within reasonable bounds and to make the divergent forces act in concert for the general welfare. This raises the question of political institutions, the most important problem facing France. The present difficulties in this sphere stem from the fact that the political institutions which were adopted in 1946 in no way satisfy the requirements of the economic, social, and political situation whose major characteristics have just been sketched.

The Problem of Institutions

French public opinion, because of the addition of new divisive forces to its many traditional political tendencies, is today more confusedly split and more unstable than it has ever been. The consequences of this fragmentation of opinion are aggravated by the substitution in almost every case of tightly organized parties for the flexible and undisciplined groups of earlier days. The investment program for the modernization of the French economy requires from every social group sacrifices which are made more acute by the fact that they are demanded at a time when French resources have been considerably depleted by the physical destruction of two wars, by the liquidation of most of France's old foreign investments, and by the flight of capital due to the depreciation of the currency. Finally, the international tension forces France to make decisive choices and additional sacrifices which further aggravate its economic position and make it more difficult to maintain a satisfactory balance of social forces. Such a situation requires democratic political institutions capable of creating a government that will be coherent, stable, and strong.

The government must be coherent because, when it is a matter of demanding sacrifices from every social category, half measures, compromises, and contradictions create too many discrepancies in the total program and offer too many possibilities for this or that social group to evade bearing its share of the sacrifices and thereby to pass it on to the others. The government must be stable because it is indispensable to renounce operating on day-to-day policies, to adopt a long-range plan of action, and to apply it courageously until it bears fruit, which by definition does not ripen quickly. The government must be strong because a parliamentary majority based on a coalition—and it is impossible to conceive of any other kind in a country whose political traditions are as stamped with diversity as France's—is always subject to pressures which may divide it if it is not kept in check and guided by a governmental team endowed with sufficient authority to keep it united. The government must also be strong because the highly technical nature of the problems which must be solved does not permit the substitution of parliamentary initiative, which is sometimes inspired by private interests, for government initiative, which can turn for aid and advice to the administrative services. The government alone is capable of considering the general welfare and of arbitrating between the contradictory claims of separate social groups because it is the only agency which can take a broad view of the situation.

The French political tradition is not conducive to satisfying these requirements. Since democracy emerged in France, the governments have almost always been divided, unstable, and weak. The first element in any study of French institutions must be to seek the causes of the chronic weakness of democratic governments in France.

The idea of democracy is complex, and its meaning can be discussed at great length. For the purposes of this analysis, however, it is not necessary to carry the discussion into its widest ramifications. It may simply be said, in the words of Abraham Lincoln, that democracy is government of the people, by the people, and for the people. To be more concrete, it can be said that a government is democratic when it is based on free universal suffrage and when it is organized so that in the event of a conflict between the separate elements among which political power is divided—and power must be divided to avoid having a dictatorship—the last word rests with the free universal suffrage. Democracy postulates the existence of more than one party, free elections, the control of the executive by one or more freely elected assemblies, the independent administration of justice, and the protection of the citizens against arbitrary acts of the government and of the police. The specific problem at hand is to determine why the democratic ideal, thus expressed, in terms which seem to be acceptable to everyone who wants a democracy in conformity with the liberal Western tradition, has never operated with practical effectiveness in France the way it has in the Anglo-Saxon countries, in Switzerland, or in the Scandinavian countries.

First of all, it seems that this ideal has never been unanimously accepted in France. For a long time it was rejected by the reactionary segment of opinion. When this group apparently rallied to democracy, it was abandoned by an important part of the extreme Left, which became converted to the Communist and antiliberal conception of "popular democracy" or "mass democracy."

The right-wing opposition to democracy for a long time revealed itself to be singularly strong. The Republic was established by the National Assembly in 1875 by a majority of only one vote. In 1877, the opponents of the Republic tried to crush it in the affair of the Sixteenth of May. Ten years later the Boulanger Movement appeared. Twelve years after that, the reactionary offensive started again on the occasion of the Dreyfus Affair. The Republic emerged from these crises victoriously, and it seemed to be planted on solid ground. But the activities and the success of the Action Française testified to the survival of the irreconcilable doctrinal chauvinism of the Republic's adversaries. During the great depression, the riot of February 6, 1934, and then the agitation of the antiparliamentary leagues—which were more or less inspired by Fascism as well as by the Maurrasian criticism of democracy—proved that democracy's enemies had not been disarmed and that they were still capable of finding an audience in an important area of opinion. At the time of France's defeat in July 1940, which for Maurras was a "divine surprise" because it provoked the collapse of the democratic republic, every act of the Vichy government—which even suppressed the very name "republic" for which it substituted the term "French State"—proved that the opponents of the principle of democracy had maintained an infinitely stronger position in important circles and in opinion than might have been generally supposed.

The extreme discredit into which the Pétain regime fell has unquestionably weakened the reactionary opposition to democracy since 1940. It has not been reorganized after the Liberation on as strong a basis as before the war, perhaps because the growth of the Communist opposition to democracy has given democracy a benevolent and protective appearance, perhaps also because many people who might have gone into the camp of the enemies of democracy have gone instead to the RPF, which cannot, on the basis of its acts, its doctrine, its program, or its leadership, be regarded as being within the tradition of the old doctrinal opposition to democratic principles. However, in certain limited circles, nostalgia for the Vichy regime and admiration for Maurras continues to be expressed; but these circles do not represent a significant political force.[2]

The long persistence of a refusal on principle to accept democracy can be explained by one of the fundamental traits of French political psychology, the penchant for coherent systems of thought,

[2] In the 1951 election this tendency was represented by the UNIR, but it elected only three deputies: M. Isorni in Paris, M. Leroy-Ladurie in Calvados, and M. de Saivre in Oran. It controls two weekly newspapers, *Aspects de la France* and *Rivarol*.

logically and carefully shaped, which pretend to give a complete account of social and human reality, and the various elements of which are so interconnected that no one of them can be abandoned without causing the collapse of the entire system. This explains the prestige of the "master thinkers" who, from de Maistre to de Bonald to Maurras, constantly persuaded part of the French public that democratic principles were not only dangerous but false.

Along with ideas, interests have had a far from negligible role in the persistence of an antidemocratic opposition in France. During the Revolution and then during the first two-thirds of the nineteenth century, attempts to establish democracy always occurred in violent form. There never was any evolutionary process as there was in Great Britain. Riots, barricades, and revolutionary episodes fomented by advocates of democracy gravely worried the propertied classes. The logic of the French mind led them to believe that the demand for social equality would necessarily follow the demand for political equality. During the Second Republic, from 1848 to 1851, such fears made people who had at first apparently rallied to the democratic cause become its most ardent opponents. In more recent times, the social reforms enacted by the Popular Front in 1936 certainly contributed to reinforcing, on the eve of the Second World War, the current of hostility to democracy which was to be unleashed under the aegis of Pétain after the Armistice of June 1940.

Religious factors, however, are the main cause of the persistence of antidemocratic doctrines. The Old Regime merged the civil and religious spheres to an extent that is difficult to understand today. The monarchy in a country that was "the eldest daughter of the Church" and whose sovereign was "the most Christian King" was not only a political system but a sort of religious institution, as attested by the coronation rites in the cathedral at Reims. Because of this interrelationship, the civil and political transformation undertaken by the Revolution could not fail to appear sacrilegious. All those, even among the lower classes, who were attached to the old "Christianity" were violently hostile to the reforms, even the political ones, which had accompanied the attempt to subvert the old privileged position of the Church. These people naturally became the irreconcilable adversaries of the democratic doctrine in whose name these reforms had been undertaken. The effect of the Revolution was to drive, at the dawn of the nineteenth century, the Church of France and the mass of its followers into the camp of the opponents of democracy. The consequences of this in French political life remain numerous: a striking example is the importance which is attached today to a problem like that of the private schools.

According to a Dominican, Father Congar,[3] "French politics, right up until today, has had a philosophical and religious significance. For a long time, Revolution meant something else than the abolition of privileges; Republic meant something else and much more than a political system; the modern world meant something else and much more than a set of living conditions and a sympathetic attitude to certain values. These broad categories, which became veritable 'myths,' contained in fact a rejection of all submission to any authority superior to the individual conscience. . . . Unfortunately, instead of joining the men . . . loyal at once to God or to the Church and to their century, like Lacordaire, many Catholics perpetuated the confusion: they either, like Lamennais, accepted without taking the time to make the necessary distinctions the totality of Jacobin ideas, or, like Veuillot and later the conservatives of the first fifty years of the Third Republic, they rejected totally the 'conquests of the modern world' and became, also without discernment, the enemies of the world in which the Church is called to work."

For a long time, many more Catholics have followed the example of Veuillot than that of Lamennais. Their hostility to democracy was founded on two convictions which seemed to them to be inseparable: one is political, the idea that a society can exist only on the basis of a hierarchy, because the masses are incapable of govern-

[3] *Vie Intellectuelle,* June 1950.

ing themselves; the other is religious, the idea that as man's nature has been corrupted by original sin he must be oriented toward good by guides, by tutors, who can only be the traditional authorities of all categories—families notable for their lineage or their wealth, established groups, technical experts, the Church, even a monarchy—from which, on the contrary, democracy seeks to emancipate the masses. These convictions produced a situation which is symbolized by this significant fact: in the current vocabulary of many of the French provinces, the word "Catholic" is quite naturally contrasted not with the words "Protestant" or "freethinker" but with the word "republican." These convictions also, because of the power retained by the Church of France, have provided the strength, which has for so long menaced democracy, of those people who, whether out of intellectual conviction, out of selfishness, out of religious belief, or out of a combination of these motives, rejected the very principle of democracy.

The existence of this opposition has greatly contributed to give to the idea of democracy, in the minds of those who were attached to it—one is tempted to say of its believers—a very special content: their fear of deviations, their desire for orthodoxy, their defensive attitude, their suspicious reaction to the acceptance of democracy by its former opponents—all flow from it. If democracy, in the minds of its advocates, has frequently appeared to be an idea, a value in itself, the practical application of which mattered less than its doctrinal purity, this also derives partially from the fact that political struggles in France during a considerable period took on the aspect of philosophic or religious controversies.

Historical circumstances have also made the idea of democracy, as it developed in France in the nineteenth century, appear in many respects to be less a concept of government than a concept of the resistance of the citizen to power and, therefore, of resistance to government. The basic cause of this negative conception of democracy is that it was formed at a time when the advocates of democracy were almost always in the opposition. "It became customary," explains the English historian David Thomson, in his penetrating essay, *Democracy in France*,[4] "to think of democracy and government as two separate poles in politics, too far apart for the vital spark of democratic government to flash between them." It is because of this that the traditional French idea of democracy is indifferent to practical accomplishments, to economic activity, to social benefits. It proclaims idealistic values, and it habitually contrasts them with the values of oligarchical or authoritarian governments. When it accedes to power, its major concern is to affirm the triumph of its values through symbolic and ideological measures, for example, by secularizing education or by separating Church and State: it does not concern itself with applying a large scale policy of production, construction, and trade. In this domain it feels incompetent; these things do not interest it; it follows un-resistingly the suggestions of special-interest groups.

This is what explains the recourse by the Third Republic to that effortless solution, protective tariff policies, an inevitable cause of economic stagnation for a country with an internal market relatively as small as that of France. "The great thing which our era of material civilization demands," André Siegfried wrote as early as 1930,[5] "must be done, in France, outside the political sphere and almost unknown to it, because our democracy, born with other preoccupations and conceived for other goals, has neither the means for nor even a genuine interest in such a program. . . . Perhaps even those 'great things,' which might have seduced Colbert or Napoleon, are in essence antidemocratic in the sense in which France understands democracy, that is, foreign to the nature of a system in which the masses do not want to organize and refuse to sacrifice the individual to the discipline from above which every great material enterprise demands."

Earlier, the Radical philosopher Alain, the author of a book with the significant title, *Le citoyen contre les pouvoirs,* said: "The real strength of the voters is defined by resistance to power rather

[4] David Thomson, *Democracy in France, the Third Republic* (London, 1946), p. 14.

[5] André Siegfried, *Tableau des partis en France* (Paris, 1930), pp. 90–91.

than by reformist action." [6] And all his political writings, consisting mainly of *Propos* written for a left-wing newspaper in Normandy, develop the theme that government is in essence reactionary because it necessarily tends to consider itself as an end in itself, that those who wield power, even if they are of democratic inspiration, are inevitably corrupted by it, and that the duty of true democrats is to control them unceasingly in order to prevent them from acting, even if their activity is "reformist." It is easy to understand why democratic governments supported by followers animated by such a spirit, and opposed obstinately by an opposition which rejected their basic principles, were never able to be very vigorous, very stable, or very active.

It is clear that such a concept of democracy could have appeared and endured only in a very special kind of society, an individualistic and static society like the one which existed in most of France in the nineteenth century and which still exists today in many parts of the country. In this context also, the regional differences in the relative strength of the parties that was demonstrated in Chapter III are important. The distinction between an economically and socially dynamic France and a static France illuminates contemporary political problems. Static France is where there are small productive units, each one complete in itself, the prosperity of which depends much more on the personal qualities of their managers than on the general conditions of the market or on the activity of the state. It has a solidarity and a capacity to resist crises, but it is also incapable of integrating itself into a great program for the expansion of production. The social groups which emerge from such an economic substructure are by nature indifferent to governmental effectiveness. This is what Robert de Jouvenel was saying when he wrote in 1914: "France is a happy land, where the soil is generous, where the craftsman is ingenious, where the wealth is divided. Here politics is a matter of taste, it is not the condition of man's existence." One could hardly explain in better terms why the idea of democracy which developed in France before the First

[6] Alain, *Eléments d'une doctrine radicale* (Paris, 1925), p. 123.

World War has a negative, purely ideological character and is so indifferent to state activity.

As has already been pointed out, however, all of France is not static. There is a dynamic France, a modern France, where the techniques of production are changing and where the social structure is in flux. This is the France of great industries and, more importantly, of dependent industries integrated into a complex economic process where individualism is no longer possible because the failure of one productive unit affects the operation of the others, instead of giving them an opportunity to enjoy even more business as is the case in static France. This dynamic France cannot be indifferent to the activity of the state because it needs an effective program of public works, of electrification, of transportation; because it is linked to international markets where its competitive position is to a large extent a function of the budgetary and fiscal policy of the state; because the problems of the levels of prices and wages are as important to it as they are unimportant to static France, where, especially in agriculture, many units employ no wage labor and consume a large part of their products themselves. The dissatisfaction of this modern France with the traditional French notion of democracy expresses itself today in the majority support it gives to the opposition parties. This dissatisfaction has for several decades already contributed toward alienating certain groups from the camp of the traditional democrats, sometimes toward the Right, sometimes toward the Left.

On the one hand, this situation has helped to strengthen the antidemocratic current by partially reviving its old arguments and by adding to them some others of a more practical kind. The unstable and ineffective democratic governments, which have been primarily concerned with ideological symbols, have alienated those who regarded their methods as inadequate and who felt the necessity for an effective administrative and economic policy. Thus some sections of the *bourgeoisie* and of business circles who had at first accepted democracy, often because it was not Catholic, ended by rejecting it, or at least by criticizing its practical application in circumstances which brought them close to the reactionary opposition, when they did not become completely identified with it. One consequence of this fusion was to facilitate the progressive adoption of democracy by some of its former adversaries, who accepted its principles while they continued to criticize the concrete form it had taken in France. This is one of the causes of the present weakness of the reactionary Right. A more important practical consequence, however, was the movement toward the Left of some of the traditional democrats, toward socialism and then toward communism.

Socialism presents itself less as an adversary of the traditional idea of democracy than as the heir to this tradition. It does not reject the political content of democracy; it claims only to complete it by establishing social democracy. It does not intend to destroy, but at most to change, the governmental and parliamentary institutions erected by the traditional democrats. It accepts, for example, the plurality of parties and free elections. But it intends to use these institutions to extend the application of democratic principles to economic and social life, and thereby to transform the conditions in which the proletarian worker spends his life. Its aim is to develop in the society created by modern industrial life the sentiments which, in the countryside and in the small cities with a precapitalistic economy, had given birth to the traditional notion of democracy. The desire for equality and liberty, which had taken on a purely political form in these static areas, acquires a social content in the modern industrialized areas. The authoritarian organization of the factories, where the hierarchy is determined by the ownership of capital, and the brutal contrast in standards of living make the society within which the workers exist one where, at a time when there is neither collective bargaining nor shop stewards and no union control that is accepted by the management, democratic principles have almost no application. Participating in the sovereignty of the state by his ballot, and consulted as a citizen on the general problems of political orientation, the wage earner in the factory feels completely excluded from its management. No one asks his advice on matters which he nevertheless understands well because they concern his daily life: the organization of the shop, the fixing of hours for work and for leisure, the method of calculating wages. Such a distortion between the principles of the political structure of the country and the realities of its social structure necessarily create tensions which are translated, with the appearance of socialism, into a desire for concrete and effective reforms. This is moving away from traditional French democracy, which is concerned, as Alain said, more with resisting power than with enacting reforms.

There was another movement away from the traditional notion of democracy, and a much more decisive one, after the First World War when the Communist party was created. For the Communists it is not a matter of extending political democracy into economic democracy. The Communists deny the value of the traditional political institutions of democracy. They consider them to be a delusion because, as the Communists emphasize the economic and social aspects of power exclusively, they deny that the right to vote of those whose material condition is precarious or dependent on others gives them an effective means of defending their interests and making those interests prevail in the conduct of public affairs. Liberal democracy, they say, is not government *for* the people because it is not truly government *by* the people. What does his ballot mean to an unemployed laborer? The Communists therefore want to destroy by revolutionary action not only capitalism but the so-called democratic state which to them seems to be in reality the tool of capitalism. Then they will institute the dictatorship of the proletariat which, heedless of the fallacious forms of liberal democracy, will get down to the heart of things and really, rather than simply formally, defend the interests of the masses and emancipate the workers. In order to realize the ideals of social democracy—justice, equality and genuine liberty—the Communists reject the methods of political democracy. For free elections in a system based on a multiplicity of parties, they want to substitute, in order to determine and apply the will of the people, the activity of a single people's party, tightly organized, capable of incarnating this will even before it has been fully expressed, because as the party consists of the most conscious and most active elements of the proletariat it constitutes its advance guard. This is government *for* the people *by the party* of the people. Based on the assumption of the infallibility of the proletarian party, and excluding any external control over its action and, therefore, over the action of the state which is in practice identified with it, this attitude confers an absolute power which is directly contrary to true democracy.

Communism has succeeded in developing considerably in France, not only among the proletariat but, as has been indicated in Chapter III, also in certain areas whose social structure might make them disposed to remain loyal to the traditional conception of democracy in its most negative sense and in its indifference to the effectiveness of state action. This goes back to the fact that the idea of the false character of purely political, liberal democracy is not unrelated to the traditional distrust of the militants of the Left for the essentially reactionary character of the government. Nor is it unrelated to their convictions about the inevitable changes that the exercise of power brings about in the democrats who attain power.

As for the development of communist ideas among the proletariat, this can undoubtedly be explained by the long, tenacious, and, to a large extent, victorious resistance of the capitalists to the efforts to establish democratic methods in the factories where the proletariat works. The improvement—which has been too slow—in the material conditions of the workers could not be enough to prevent many of them from separating themselves from a democratic idea which appeared to have no real grasp of the basic problems of their lives.

In spite of the increasing importance that the political currents dissatisfied with the traditional French conception of democracy assumed during the period between the two World Wars, the institutions of the Third Republic had not been changed in a way that might increase their effectiveness, by giving to the government more authority, coherence, and viability than it had had before the First World War. The wave of hostility to the constitutional laws of 1875 which developed after the Liberation was due to a widespread belief that those laws were responsible for the weakening of France and for the defeat of 1940. But the new constitution essentially reproduces, in aggravated form, the faults of the old one.

There are several reasons for this. The Communist party, which wanted to destroy liberal democracy, had every reason for introducing elements of weakness into the institutions of the French Republic by multiplying excessively the prerogatives of the National Assembly to the detriment of those of the cabinet. The Socialist party had appeared anxious to strengthen the structure of the democratic state; several books published by some of its most eminent leaders [7] before the election of the Constituent Assembly created the impression that it would support endowing the cabinet with the powers it needs to carry out its duties. But actually, in the constitutional sphere as in others, efforts to renew the Socialist doctrine produced no results. The desire to remain faithful to the orthodoxy established by its founders forty years earlier—before two World Wars and their economic and social consequences had completely altered the facts of French political life; the fear of not being far enough "to the Left" and of suffering the criticism of the Communists; the lack of imagination and experience of their provincial militants, who had the power to impose their views on their most qualified leaders because of the rules for the organization of the party—all this led the Socialist party to contribute decisively to making the Fourth Republic's political system one of government by assembly rather than a real parliamentary system, balanced and efficient.

The doctrinaire opposition of the Catholics to democracy had just about disappeared after the Liberation. The creation and the

[7] For example, Léon Blum, *A' l'échelle humaine,* and Vincent Auriol, *Hier et demain.*

success of the MRP symbolized their acceptance of social and political democracy. But this fact, so fortunate in other respects, was not favorable for the erection of a stronger political system than that of the Third Republic. Politically, the MRP, after the rejection of the first constitutional draft at the referendum of May 5, 1946, did not believe it was possible to continue to struggle against the ideas of the Socialists and the Communists. The party therefore accepted compromises which favored assembly government. Psychologically, the Christian Democratic militants too often suffer from a sort of inferiority complex, and fearing to be regarded as weak democrats, they failed to demand sufficient powers for the cabinet. Doctrinally, their conception of society did not favor the creation of an effective state structure. The MRP, following the line of thought of certain Catholic philosophers, felt that the various natural groups of which human society consists —families, towns, trades or professions, churches, etc.—all possessed, by natural law, a private area of activity in which the state must not intervene. Their fear of the encroachments of a Jacobin, omnipotent state prevented them from understanding the necessity for a strong state. They hoped to overcome the individualism of the Third Republic by "organizing" democracy through the new role conferred on political parties and by complicated legal mechanisms (contrived by professors of constitutional law with inventive minds but with inadequate experience), such as the investiture of the Premier prior to the formation of the cabinet, the requirement of a delay before taking the vote on motions of censure or confidence, and the requirement of special majorities for certain decisions. In practice, these mechanisms were to be unworkable or harmful.

The conservatives and the Radicals, who were in favor essentially of maintaining the institutions of the Third Republic, had too few deputies in the Constituent Assemblies to be able to play an effective role in the establishment of the institutions of the Fourth Republic.

These institutions reveal very clearly the fear of personal power which haunted many politicians of all beliefs, at a time when General de Gaulle had just resigned from power. Only this fear can explain why, despite the verbal agreement given by various sides as to the need of strengthening the executive, the executive was definitely made weaker than it had been during the Third Republic. Moreover, the interim regime established in 1945–1946, during the discussion of the constitution, was by necessity a system of assembly government, and many of its characteristics were to be carried over into the permanent political structure.

The rules of parliamentary procedure followed by the Constituent Assemblies were adopted by the National Assembly after the constitution went into operation, and these were essentially the same as those followed during the Third Republic. Although this aspect of the problem is often disregarded by people who study the problem of institutional reform, the standing orders of the Assemblies are perhaps more important than the constitution in shaping the real character of a political system. The fact that the constitution prescribed no general rules for the organization of the National Assembly, except to require that its officers be elected on the basis of proportional representation of the various groups and to state that proposed legislation will be studied in committees, contributed largely to the reappearance under the Fourth Republic of the major faults of the declining years of the Third Republic. The chief defects of the system established in 1946 include the electoral system, the relationship between the National Assembly and the cabinet, and parliamentary procedure.

There is no necessity for discussing again at length the electoral system which has already been discussed in Chapter II. It was demonstrated there why proportional representation with blocked lists was adopted by the Fourth Republic, both as a way of increasing the role of organized parties in political life and as a common guarantee for the parties that no one of them would dominate the others. It has also been explained how the initial system was changed in 1951 by making provision for alliances and by the re-establishment of the majority principle where a single list of candidates or a group of allied lists won an absolute majority of the votes.

Both these systems have two major disadvantages. The first is that they give excessive authority to the executive committees of the parties. Only two French parties have a large membership, the RPF and the Communist party. The RPF certainly has several hundred thousand members, and the Communist party, which at one time claimed more than a million members, must certainly have about 800,000. But both these parties have an authoritarian structure which gives to the local party workers an extremely small voice in the determination of their tactics. The Socialist party and the MRP both have fewer than 200,000 members, and the Radical Socialist party has about 50,000. The practical result of this is that in every case it is an oligarchy which determines party policy and imposes it more or less rigorously on its deputies. The deputies, who are in more direct contact with their constituents and who are sensitive to the fluctuations in opinion among them, would often be less inclined to intransigence than the local party workers; but the electoral system obliges the deputies to consider first of all what the local party workers think. Such a mechanism is faulty in that it is hardly democratic, and it is all the more troublesome in France, where the local militants of the parties are doctrinaire theoreticians who are attached much more firmly than the voters are to specific traditions and orthodoxies.

The second disadvantage of the electoral system comes from this doctrinaire character of the local party militants. Spontaneous cleavages in public opinion are artificially crystallized by the intervention of the parties which are enabled by proportional representation to remain isolated. This makes the formation of coalition majorities difficult, although they are indispensable to the operation of the political system; and sometimes it makes it almost impossible for the government to follow a coherent policy. To these inherent disadvantages of proportional representation, the electoral system adopted in 1951 has added the complication that it gives the impression that the votes are being unfairly manipulated and threatens to alienate the public from a system which does not follow the rules of fair play.

The first reform that should be made in order to regenerate the institutions of the Fourth Republic is to return to a majority electoral system with two ballots, in conformity with the habits of the French voters, a simple principle with uncontestable results. But it would not be desirable to adopt this system for single-member electoral districts. For the single-member constituency leads to negative coalitions and produces no real harmony between the parties which coalesce at the second ballot by withdrawing all their candidates except one. It is the list system which should be adopted, operating under the majority principle with two ballots, and each electoral district should elect not more than four or five deputies so that there will not be an exaggerated underrepresentation of minorities. With this system, neighboring parties can form coalition lists on the second ballot, and each party can have a number of candidates included on the list corresponding to the number of votes which, judging from the results of the first ballot, it can be expected to contribute to the coalition list. The coalition list is automatically compelled to defend a common governmental program before the voters, and this in turn compels the parties to tone down what divides them and to emphasize what unites them, something that the 1951 system of alliances did not do at all. A real solidarity would be created between the deputies of various parties who were elected on the same list by the same voters. This identity of electoral interest would facilitate the formation in Parliament of a coherent and stable governing majority.

This system, which should also give the voter freedom to split his ticket and to reject specific candidates on the lists without having to reject them all, would give to personality factors the importance they should have in an election. It would not, on the other hand, abolish completely the role of organized parties (which is what might happen if the single-member-district system were used), as the parties would always have the job of preparing the coalition lists. The system, therefore, would satisfy the partial truth of the idea that democracy must be organized by parties capable both of completing the political education of the voters and of informing the political leaders of the requirements of the various sectors of the population. It also takes into consideration the irrevocable aspects of the evolutionary process which is increasing the role of parties. For the increased importance of parties represents the collectivization of political life, which is only one aspect of the more general tendency of modern civilization to take on a collective character, whether it be in the sphere of production, recreation, scientific research, or politics.

The relationships between the National Assembly and the cabinet, as they have been established by the constitution of 1946, are badly out of balance. The Assembly continually has the government at its mercy, while the government can apply on the Assembly only the instruments of persuasion. Before a cabinet can be formed, the Premier who has been designated by the President must be invested by an absolute majority of the members of the National Assembly, although for ordinary legislation the necessary majority is simply a majority of those deputies voting. In the minds of the constitution-makers this method of investiture would confer increased personal authority on the Premier and take the place of the debate on general policy which, according to the old practice, was held after the formation of the cabinet and concluded by a vote of confidence. In fact, the "presentation" of the ministry always takes place, and there are now two obstacles to be overcome instead of only one. But the majority needed for investiture is so difficult to obtain that it is not inconceivable that some day this requirement might completely paralyze the functioning of the political machinery.

According to the constitution, the government is compelled to resign only when, one full day after the motion has been introduced, the Assembly passes a vote of censure against the government or refuses to pass a motion of confidence introduced by the government; and a vote of censure can be passed or a motion of confidence rejected only by an absolute majority of the members of the National Assembly. The intention of the framers of this provision was to reduce the number of ministerial crises. The effect has been nothing of the sort. When the question of confidence is posed on a bill, the bill can be rejected by a majority of those voting, which does not constitute a majority of the members of the Assembly. In this case, confidence is not refused constitutionally, but, politically, the government is defeated; no longer having a majority behind it, it is required to resign. In addition, nothing prevents a government from resigning after an adverse vote on an issue which it has not made a formal question of confidence. Nor is there anything to prevent it from resigning without any vote at all in the Assembly, but simply because its members can no longer agree with one another; this is the reason why most of the crises of the Fourth Republic have occurred.

The failure of the procedures devised in 1946 for the purpose of enforcing government stability is striking. The only effective device in this sphere would be to grant the government the unconditional right to dissolve the National Assembly and appeal to the voters when a conflict arises between the Assembly and the government, which would mean in practice whenever the majority which started out by supporting the government became divided. It would still be necessary, however, in order to make the practice of dissolution effective, to have an electoral system conducive to the creation of a coherent majority.

But the constitution of 1946 makes the right of dissolution subject to conditions that are incapable of being realized. It becomes possible only eighteen months after the opening of a legislature, and on the condition that two ministerial crises occur within an eighteen month period as a consequence of a vote of censure or of a rejected vote of confidence passed by an absolute majority of the members of the National Assembly. The resignation of the cabinet as a consequence of internal disagreement or of an adverse vote in the Assembly that does not muster an absolute majority of all the deputies do not count as crises contributing toward making dissolution possible. Crises occurring less than fifteen days after the appointment of the ministers do not count either. These are the reasons why the National Assembly could not have been dissolved at any given moment during the first legislature although there was a ministerial crisis on the average of every five and one half months! There is really no effective dissolution power in the institutional framework created in 1946 and this is the major cause of the weakness of the executive. Subjected to the control of the Assembly, the executive has no power with which it might compensate for its dependent position. This is the basic error in the French institutional structure, and the one which any constitutional revision, if it is to be effective, must first of all rectify.

The chief defect of French parliamentary procedure is the excessive importance it confers on committees, appointed on the basis of proportional representation of the various parliamentary groups, and on the report which must precede the discussion of every bill. This is a fundamental characteristic of the French parliamentary system which harks back to the revolutionary Assemblies, and its disadvantages are enormous, although they have never really been emphasized by those people who have studied the operation of French institutions.[8]

According to this procedure, a matter can be discussed only after it has been reported on by the "competent" committee, and the text submitted to the Assembly is not that of the original bill but that of the counterproject drafted by the committee. This system actually substitutes parliamentary initiative for governmental initiative. But the technical character of the problems of legislation requires the committees to seek documentation from the administration and to be aided by the civil servants. This does

[8] Toward the end of his life, Raymond Poincaré published several articles criticizing the "committee system." But he was especially concerned over the fact that the committees were permanent and had general jurisdiction over a subject. He recommended using the old system of special committees for each bill, which had been gradually abandoned between 1880 and 1910 (the date of the establishment of the present system). Now, for practical reasons, special committees are not possible because of the large number of bills.

not reinforce the position of the government, however, for the civil servants, who are administrative personnel and not officially attached to the Assemblies, to whom the committees turn for aid are generally not the same people who have worked on the preparation of the initial bills introduced by the government. This system permits, or rather provokes, the development of hostile cliques within the administration; it weakens the discipline and the authority of the ministers who have practically no control over the members of their staffs "on detached service" with the parliamentary committees. The result is a serious dilution of responsibilities which enables interest groups to intervene effectively, but discreetly, in the preparation of legislation.

The rule which prohibits any debate from taking place without a committee report has the same effect; no one knows who is responsible when a problem is not settled. Once the government has introduced a bill it cannot force the committee to issue its report. The committee can prolong its work indefinitely and justify its delay by saying that the government has not sent it all the documentation it needs. The Assembly cannot, according to its rules, start the discussion without the report. No one is really guilty of paralyzing the governmental machinery because responsibility is shared and no one has the power to make the others discharge their share of the responsibility.

Once the committee has issued its report, the problem remains of having the matter included in the agenda, which is fixed by the Assembly and which is always too full. The Government's desires must be heard but in this case, as in all the others, the government can employ only the power of persuasion.

Slowness, inefficiency, disorder, and dispersion of responsibility are inevitable consequences of such procedure. The situation is rendered even more exasperating because the Presidents of the Assemblies are poorly armed against obstruction manifested by the multiplication of incidental motions, amendments, and lengthy speeches.

The fundamental reforms which must be enacted in this sphere are to give the government the right to establish the agenda of the Assembly, perhaps for two-thirds of its sittings, with the remaining one-third left to the Assembly for exercising its duty of control through questions or interpellations as well as for the discussion of private members' bills. Discretionary power should be confided to the President of the Assembly to give, take away, or refuse the floor and to accept or to reject the discussion of amendments. The "guillotine" procedure, the prior arrangement of the length of time for the discussion of a bill after which a vote must be taken, should be established.

By way of preparing the Assembly for making its final decision, the present committee stage should be replaced by two successive readings, the first of which would take place without formality, perhaps before an unspecialized committee of the Assembly, the members of which would be chosen by lot and replaced frequently. The debate would be opened, in committee and in plenary session, by the minister concerned with the bill, and not by a *rapporteur*, and the debate should take place on the initial text of the bill. The deputies could amend the bill, of course, but on their own responsibility and without having their counterproposals enjoy the favorable blessings of having been adopted by a supposedly competent committee.

The practice of having reports prepared by a committee should be retained, however, for private members' bills, which are generally so hastily drafted by their authors that it would be impossible to submit them in their original form for the decision of the Assembly. The committees would also retain a *raison d'être* as they would be the organs of the *a posteriori* control of Parliament over the acts of the government.

Such a system would be perfectly democratic because it would leave intact the power of decision of Parliament, which would remain free to amend or to reject the government's bills. But it would re-establish the authority of the government by restoring to it the initiative which, for technical reasons and in order to maintain the consistency of the laws, should belong to the government.

The question arises of whether it would be appropriate to go even farther and re-establish the possibility, which existed during the Third Republic, of the Parliament's delegating its legislative power to the government for a specified period and for more or less clearly defined purposes. The advocates of this system, called the decree-law system, point out that certain unpopular but indispensable measures can be enacted in detail by Parliament only with great difficulty, but that Parliament can confide them to the government to carry out. The practice is unfortunate for it implies the flight of the Assemblies from responsibilities which they find it difficult to accept. In certain cases where speed and discretion are necessary, decree-laws can be defended. On the whole, however, if the necessary balance between the Parliament and the cabinet were established, and if the cabinet were given, by reforms in the legislative procedure as described above, the powers which it lacks today to defend its proposals and to get them adopted by Parliament, the necessity for the decree-law system would be felt far less than it is now. The decree-law system is really a reaction to the paralysis of Parliament; it would not seem to be necessary if Parliament were organized so that it could function properly. At most, it would be appropriate to confine the language of the laws to general principles, leaving the details necessary for their application to be fixed by governmental directives. If, however, French political institutions were to remain in the state in which they exist today, or were to be tinkered with only on points of detail, like changing the procedure for investing the Premier, then recourse to the decree-law procedure might easily turn out to be necessary as a compensation for the paradox of an omnipotent Parliament rendered impotent by the scope of its tasks and by the fact that it is naturally not designed to deal with many of them.

What has been said earlier in this study about the reasons why

the traditional conception of democracy, and even the whole notion of political democracy, have been repudiated by the people
who today place their confidence in communism implies that a
reform of the political institutions, however indispensable it is,
is not enough. The re-establishment in France of a unanimity of
public opinion about the true nature of democratic values will be
accomplished only when these values have been extended to the
professional and social spheres. A detailed study of the methods
which might be followed in this respect would go beyond the scope
of the present study. It must be indicated, however, that the problem exists. The adoption by a group like the RPF of the principle
of the association of capital and labor proves that people are
aware of this problem even in areas of opinion that are foreign
to doctrinaire socialism.

The aim of the nationalization of key industries which took
place in France after the Liberation was not only the destruction
of a certain economic "feudalism" which had exerted undesirable
pressure on the state after the First World War but also to make
the proletariat conscious that French democracy was going to become social democracy. This was also the goal of the establishment
of shop committees in the factories. It cannot be said that these
reforms have been successful. Their failure is due in part to the
activities of the Communist controlled unions, which participated
in putting them into effect and which then did everything they
could to prevent them from appeasing the discontent created over
a period of several decades by an autocratic economic structure.
They acted this way because the Communist party, which considers the class struggle to be the essential factor in its revolutionary activity cannot accept anything which tends to attenuate it.

It is likely, on the other hand, that the transfer of ownership of
the factories to the state is hardly enough to satisfy the aspirations
of the workers to social democracy. It is not through a transfer of
ownership, but by reform of the internal structure of all enterprises employing a significant number of wage earners that the
solution of the problem must be approached. Experiments have

already been started in this respect in various enterprises. Their results, which vary in degrees of success, are nevertheless almost always encouraging. It should be the task of a government, operating within a reorganized institutional framework which would give it the capacity to carry out a long-range program, to give new impetus to these experiments, to co-ordinate them, and to draw conclusions as to their effectiveness. When circumstances warranted it, the government could make compulsory the universal application of the system which had been demonstrated to be valuable.

The problem of the reform of the organization of industry is, in its technical aspects, beyond the personal competence of the author.[9] This is why only its existence is indicated here. It is linked, however, to the more general problem of restoring effective democracy in France through institutional changes, for the latter will not suffice in themselves, however necessary they are, if the entire public is not persuaded that democracy is more than a façade. The task is to make democracy a living reality in the daily existence of each citizen.

The Problem of the Majority

The Center majority, which was victorious in the election of June 17, 1951, suffered so many serious blows during the summer and fall parliamentary sessions that the question arises of whether it might not be more effective to replace it with a majority of a different orientation than to try to solder it together again. It broke not only over the school question but, at the time of the interpellations over economic policy in November, the Pleven government won a vote of confidence only because of the abstention of the Socialists. The reconstitution of this majority in December, for the vote on the ratification of the Schuman plan for

[9] On this subject, see the superb report on the reform of industry prepared for the Economic Council by Professor Georges Lasserre (*Journal Officiel, Edition des Avis et Rapports du Conseil Economique, Année 1950*, March 24). The acount of the discussion of this report appeared in *Bulletin du Conseil Economique*, March 23, 1950.

the European Community for Coal and Steel, although it was encouraging, produced no further consequences. In January 1952, when the cabinet made a question of confidence of the articles of the finance law which would have authorized the government to reorganize the management of the state-owned French railroads and the social-security system by decree, within the framework of certain defined principles and in order to realize economies in their operation, the Socialists joined the Communist and Gaullist opposition and caused the cabinet's collapse. The discord between the Center parties is therefore not limited to the purely political problems involved in the religious question; it also involves economic, financial, and social policy.

The Moderates and many of the Radicals actually believe that the budgetary difficulties are due essentially to the reforms enacted after the Liberation. They claim to be resolved not to accept any new taxes unless economy measures are undertaken in the management of the nationalized industries—i.e., the railroads, which have been nationalized longest, since 1938, and which are the only nationalized industry running at a deficit—and of the social-security system. The Socialists, however, are afraid that these measures will affect the remuneration or the pensions of the railroad workers and of the employees of the social-security system. Born defenders of all wage earners, they oppose reorganization at the same time that they fear that the pretext of taking economy measures really camouflages a desire for political and social revenge on the part of the opponents of the post-Liberation reforms. The reasons why the Socialists, in agreement on this question with most of the MRP, want to apply a sliding wage scale, which the Moderates and the Radicals fear will generate inflation, are identical with the reasons why they oppose reforms in the railroad and social-security systems. The Socialist militants believe that their party will be able to attract the mass of the people, and especially the working-class element, only if it stops making the concessions to the liberal parties which it has had to make between 1947 and 1951. They have "opposition fever," which is intensified by the belief that in case the liberal economic policy fails they will be able, as an opposition party, to prevent the Communist party from benefiting from the political consequences of that failure. The question remains, however, given the present balance of political forces, can another majority than that of June 17, 1951, which runs from the Moderates to the Socialists, be formed in the National Assembly?

In the absence of a Center majority, is it conceivable that a majority including the Communist party could be formed? The answer is no. The breach between Communists and non-Communists has now become by far the widest of all those which divide the various sectors of opinion. In the cantonal elections of October 1951 there was no attempt to unite the anticlerical Communists, Socialists, and Radical-Socialists against the proclericals, except in about fifty small rural cantons, out of more than 1,500. Nevertheless, in the areas least advanced economically, where politics is thought of according to the categories of the nineteenth century, there would have been no better basis than anticlericalism for re-establishing the old Union of the Left. The methods of the Communist party, the complete subjection it displays to the Cominform, and the incredible excesses of its polemics have placed it completely apart from French political life. It exists as a sort of foreign body (the party as such, not its voters),[10] still of impressive strength despite its decline at the 1951 elections, but organically incapable of participating in harmonious community life. Furthermore, even if these decisive obstacles did not exist, the debates over the school laws proved that the Left, in the now obsolete sense

---

[10] A public opinion poll taken at the end of 1950 (cited by Claude Bourdet in *l'Observateur* of December 21, 1950) estimated at 32 per cent the percentage of voters disposed at that time to vote Communist, but at only 13 per cent those who would favor the U.S.S.R. in case of a Russo-American war. The difference between the two figures shows that electoral support of communism does not, by far, reflect complete adherence to its doctrine and its policies. The Communist vote more often reflects an unbreakable habit of voting for the extreme Left, or a vague and easily explained discontent, rather than a genuine conviction.

that the word had fifty years ago, does not possess a majority in the National Assembly.

The transformation of the coalition which voted for the Barangé school bill into a governing majority extending to all current problems is no less impossible. The MRP cannot, without renouncing its individuality, become a participant in a socially conservative bloc after having had to appear the leader of the right-wing majority, in the old religious sense of the word, which formed on the private-school issue. There is no reason to believe, moreover, that the RPF, which is also wary of appearing as the heir of the old Right, would agree to participate in so small and so precarious a majority. Its *raison d'être* requires it to try for something more and better.

There is another hypothesis, dear to the socially conservative, which envisages a simultaneous split in the RPF and the MRP which would contribute from two directions enough support to a core of Moderates and Radicals to transform it into a governing majority. Of all the theoretical possibilities discussed so far, this is undoubtedly the only one which could conceivably occur in fact. But it is unlikely that it will come about: there have been few signs of schism until now either in the Gaullist bloc or in the MRP. The strength which the organized parties have acquired under the Fourth Republic tends to remove from the area of possibility a solution which, before 1939, would have had a good chance to succeed. Unless the majority electoral system with two ballots and with single-member districts were to be revived—which might break up the parties—this hypothetical majority does not seem viable.

The Moderates, who would be the happiest over Gaullist participation in the government, want the entrance of the RPF into the government to be the cause of a split in the RPF itself. Their plan is to appeal to certain members of the RPF parliamentary group to enter the government, but to exclude De Gaulle himself. The Gaullists, however, would regard their participation in a Right-Center ministry under the premiership of a Moderate, a

Popular Republican, or a Radical as only the first step in De Gaulle's return to power. The RPF considers that such a ministry would be only a transitional government which would have to enact a majority electoral law and make some preliminary revisions of the constitution. Then the National Assembly would be dissolved, and the Gaullists think that new elections would give them a decisive majority which would enable them to govern alone. Considered by some as a step toward the dissociation of the RPF and by others as a step toward its total victory, this majority which some politicians would like to see crystallize, oriented toward the Right, and consisting of the RPF, the Moderates, the Radicals, and some Popular Republicans, seems to be mortgaged with such contradictions in its origin that its realization is highly doubtful.

This being the nature of the impasse—no extreme Left majority, no right-wing majority similar to the one which passed the school laws, no coalition majority extending from the RPF to the Radicals and augmented by the most conservative Popular Republicans—is it likely that there will be a break in political tradition and a general realignment of parties capable of creating a new type of majority? Such a majority, and nothing is more obvious, would have to include the RPF, the Socialist party, and the MRP, the three political groups which are animated, in different ways, by the same desire to regenerate France. These three parties might be joined by some of the Moderates and Radicals who are aware of the fundamental changes that have taken place in the nature of French political problems since the Second World War.

This majority could be produced only out of the desire of the leaders of every shade of opinion to put the problem on a higher level than that of the customary rivalry between parties and to form a *rassemblement* for the purpose of achieving, without doctrinaire and partisan wrangling over methods, a certain number of goals which are obviously directly related to the general welfare. Such goals would include the reconstruction of political institutions; stopping inflation; improving the conditions of the working masses; rearmament within the framework of the Atlantic Pact in concurrence with France's allies, but without French submission to external decisions; and speeding the constitution of a European federation of nations faithful to Western democracy.

It is advisedly that the word *rassemblement* has been used to define the form that such a majority would have to take. It is the author's view that the evidence demonstrates that General de Gaulle's attempt, made in 1947, to "rally" the French, although it undoubtedly was premature and unskillfully executed, corresponds to the only way in which it is today possible to escape from the impasse into which French democracy has strayed.

De Gaulle was once called "a political soothsayer;" he sees things clearly *at long range*. But he does not understand the *current* conditions for the success of the policies which he feels are necessary. The creation of the RPF in 1947 was the best confirmation of this judgment. Conditions were not ripe for a real *rassemblement* right after the collapse of tripartism, at a time when the disadvantages of proportional representation, the defects of the institutions created in 1946, and the impossibility of maintaining a Third Force majority were not yet clearly understood by the public. De Gaulle's action has not had the effects which he expected because the initiative was premature and because it was made without prior consultation with the Socialist and Popular Republican leaders, or with the leaders of the noncommunist trade unions, when it was of the utmost importance that these people not oppose the RPF at the very start. The resulting transformation of the RPF into a political party as rigid and as closed, if not more rigid and more closed, than the others which it denounces as harmful; and the creation in many social and political circles of a hostile reaction to Gaullism based on the "republican tradition"—make the creation of a true *rassemblement* considerably more difficult. If such a *rassemblement* is necessary—and the attempt has been made above to demonstrate that no other effective solution is conceivable—the force of events would work in its favor. It would still be essential, however, for the groups which would be called upon to form such a majority to become aware of its necessity and of the conditions which would hasten its formation.

The RPF would have, first of all, to give up the tactical and doctrinal stubbornness which it has until now displayed and which is contrary to its initial goals. It is correct in believing that the first problem to settle is the institutional one. The program it has adopted in this sphere is in many respects excellent; but in addition to recommending appropriate measures for creating a true parliamentary system in which the executive and Parliament would be balanced, with the cabinet responsible to Parliament but also having the power of dissolution, it proposes creating an excessively powerful presidency which would be too independent of Parliament, as the President would not be elected by the Parliament alone, but by Parliament in conjunction with delegates of the departmental and municipal councils. This presidency has obviously been tailored to fit General de Gaulle. But to establish it would be to create a dualism between the Premier and the President which might create serious difficulties and, more importantly still, it would lend itself to the accusation of dictatorship which, in a country like France, can be extremely dangerous.

The constitutional program of the RPF could, however, serve as the basis for the reforms that a true *rassemblement* should enact in order to restore the authority of the state. But in order to make the *rassemblement* possible the RPF would have to stop practicing a policy of systematic opposition, a *politique du pire* which is illustrated by its denunciation of the sliding wage scale at the same time that it voted for the bill purely for the purpose of creating a ministerial crisis, and by its opposition to the Schuman Plan. This policy can only enlarge the barriers which separate it from the other parties.

The opposition of the RPF generally would have to be less partisan than it has been until now. In fiscal and financial matters especially, how can a party which wants to be a government party associate itself with the people who pretend that it is possible to balance by economies a budget which is smaller than it was before the Second World War, in spite of the inclusion of allocations for investments that are obviously necessary? Should it take a stubborn position hostile to any increase in taxes when the austerity policy which France, just like England, must follow, the maintenance of France's independence, and the multiplicity of burdens which weigh on France's economy because of the necessity for modernization and rearmament can be dealt with satisfactorily only through increasing tax revenues?

In the field of foreign policy, if it is legitimate for the RPF to express its fears over the attitude of the government which it regards, and not without justification, as being too weak at home to be able effectively to defend France's interests abroad, the RPF should nevertheless avoid extreme language and certain exaggerated accusations which constitute both new causes of weakness in the French government's position in its relations with foreign countries and new obstacles to the *rassemblement* which must some day be produced between Gaullism and the parties now in power. To create a *rassemblement,* the RPF must, in short, give up its demand for the unconditional surrender of the elements which must eventually join hands with it. It must avoid ultimatums, and it must agree to open on a basis of equality the indispensable negotiations with its future partners.

The RPF must, lastly, understand the extent to which French political tradition is opposed to the idea of the personal rule of one man. Too often it appears as if the sole objective of the RPF were to establish General de Gaulle at the head of the state under circumstances which would provide no limitations on his authority. It is quite clear that this prospect can only deeply disturb the people who would be his associates, just as it disturbs many conservatives who would like to see the RPF contribute to the creation of a conservative majority.

These are the principal difficulties which stand in the way of the formation of a governmental majority including the RPF.

They are not created by the program of the RPF but by its methods, by the too large role it reserves for its leader in the institutions which it proposes, and, especially, by the way in which it seems to envisage setting them up for the conduct of public affairs.

Equally conciliatory efforts must be made by the Center parties. The RPF has too wide a popular support in the country for authentic democrats to have the right to refuse absolutely to cooperate with it. The Socialists were too hasty in 1947 in opposing the Gaullist movement because they found that it furnished them with a sort of alibi, or symmetrical justification, for the break they were making at the same time with the Communists. The Popular Republicans also have appeared at certain times to be exploiting their condemnation of the RPF as a sort of proof of their left-wing position and of their republicanism. These understandable but hardly magnanimous tactics are not in keeping with the requirements of the times. The days are gone when democracy could seek to protect itself by forming majorities "for the defense of the Republic" in the face of reactionary offensives like that of the *Boulangistes* in 1888, of the nationalistic anti-Dreyfusards of 1898–1899, or of the antiparliamentary leagues of 1934–1936. The problems at issue in the rivalry of parties today are vital problems of an economic, social, and international character, while those of earlier days only partially and superficially involved the existence of the nation. Today's problems cannot be trifled with.

The left-wing parties—whether the Socialists, the Popular Republicans or the Herriot-type Radicals—often reproach the RPF less for its objectives than for its methods; they acknowledge willingly that General de Gaulle has no intentions hostile to the Republic, but they are afraid that he will be condemned to endanger the Republic by circumstances and by the character of some of his electoral support. The best way to remove this danger would be not to leave the reactionaries a monopoly of influence in the RPF or a monopoly of opportunity to coalesce with it. These left-wing parties should drop their prejudice against the RPF and try to reach an agreement with it in good faith. They would not have to make any concessions on the basic principles of parliamentary democracy which, it must be recognized, are not seriously threatened by the essential features of the RPF's constitutional program.

The leaders of the RPF (as well as the worthiest elements of its rank and file), the Socialists, and the Popular Republicans are linked by many memories of the Resistance, of the struggle waged in common against the invader and against the antidemocratic regime of Vichy. It must be possible for them to discover a certain fundamental area of political beliefs which they share. Each of them feels this, but until now none has had the courage to allow this community of sentiments to be expressed over the din of prejudice, resentment, and mutual distrust which arose after January 1946. Someday it will be necessary to let the factors of unity overcome the factors of division if the French parties want to set off the liberating spark that will be required by the paralysis of the parliamentary machinery. For this paralysis threatens to occur on account of the cleavages in the Center majority, if the MRP and the Socialists continue obstinately to refuse to come to terms with the RPF or if the RPF persists in seeking to create the *rassemblement* by methods which make it impossible.

It is probable that the collaboration of the RPF with the MRP and with the Socialists, which the author regards as the only solution of the difficulties which face French political life today, would provoke the abandonment of Gaullism by some of its most reactionary elements, the people who joined it because they saw in it an effective weapon with which to wage war on the Left and not in order to create a genuine national *rassemblement* above partisan discord. This would restore to the RPF its true form, and on the national level as well as on the local level, in the area of relationships between the militants of the different parties, it would strengthen the ties between the RPF and the parties which should become its partners. Those Moderates and Radicals who have their eyes focused only on a dead past would form, with the reactionaries who would leave the RPF if the RPF were to come to

terms with the MRP and the Socialists, a minority right-wing opposition which would undoubtedly be too small, even if it merged
its votes with those of the Communists, seriously to disturb the
activity of the government of the *rassemblement.*

Sociologically, this new majority would rest less exclusively than
do the Center combinations now in power on the nonindustrial
and less-productive areas which constitute what has been referred
to in this study as static France. The RPF's strength in the cities
and in dynamic France, added to the weaker but nevertheless substantial position of the MRP in these regions, would permit the
rassemblement to end the present distinction between the center
of political gravity and the center of economic gravity of the
country. That would not be, judging things from a more exalted
point of view than that of electoral and parliamentary politics,
the least of the advantages that would stem from the realignment
of parties which, however difficult it will be to bring about, should
not be impossible to create and which would constitute, everything
considered, the most effective way of solving within the framework of a democratic system the problem of the balance of existing political forces.

It is certain, however, that at the beginning of 1952 the conditions for the realignment of parties which has just been sketched
are far from being realized. The RPF has not abandoned its
politique du pire, its systematic opposition, or its unconsidered ex-
altation of General de Gaulle. The Popular Republicans and the
Socialists have not learned that instead of trying to defend the
interests of the workers and to apply an effective economic policy
in collaboration with the Right Center, something which experience should tell them cannot produce adequate solutions of the
problems to be solved, they would do better to abandon the idea
of defending the Republic by obsolete formulas and to consider
carefully the conditions of an agreement with the RPF.

This is the reason why, for the lack of any other conceivable
solution, the Center majority, which broke on January 7, 1952,
with the collapse of the Pleven government, seemed to reappear

on January 17 when Edgar Faure was invested as Premier by all the groups in the National Assembly except the Gaullists and the Communists. But the refusal of the Socialist party to authorize its members to participate in the new government and the continued division of the majority on every basic problem hardly provide a basis for the hope that this reformulation of the same majority will be durable and effective. At the very best, the Faure cabinet will be able to get the finance law passed and it will, perhaps, be able to secure an equivocal compromise over the sliding wage scale. But it cannot take the coherent and continued action that is necessary in the spheres of constitutional reform and economic policy. For some time, the Center majority will perhaps succeed, for better or for worse, in carrying out the daily business of government, but not from the perspective of any broad view of the problems and without governmental stability. It is not certain that such methods can be tolerated for very long.

It is possible that there will eventually be an apparently insoluble ministerial crisis followed by a long succession of vain attempts to invest a Premier, and that because of this situation the non-Communist and nonreactionary groups which are today divided will become aware of the crying necessity for viewing France's problems differently from the way they have been viewed for five years, will break with their doctrinaire attitudes and paralyzing intransigence, and will finally dare to do something new in order to save French democracy. It is by no means certain that events will work out this way, but the hypothesis is not impossible. One may even be persuaded of its probability, by the memory of the extent, effectiveness, and suddenness of the political revival and the restoration of enthusiasm in public opinion which occurred on several occasions during the Third Republic, especially at the time of the Sacred Union of 1914 and when monetary and financial recovery was brought about by the government of National Union of Raymond Poincaré in 1926.

Epilogue

A FEW weeks after the preceding pages were written, the French political situation changed greatly, in circumstances that were unexpected and which for that reason require comment. That is the purpose of this epilogue. After recounting briefly the events which occurred, an attempt will be made to analyze their significance and to discuss the prospects that they hold for the future.

The Formation and Success of the Pinay Government

The cabinet of Edgar Faure, formed at the end of January 1952, was unable to overcome the contradictions which had overwhelmed its predecessor. In spite of the opposition of the Communists and the Gaullists, who were joined on this occasion by certain members of all the other groups, the Faure government obtained from the National Assembly a vote favoring, in principle, the European Defense Community, on the conditions that precautions be taken concerning the German rearmament which it implies and that before the treaty goes into effect a final effort be made in the Disarmament Commission of the United Nations to try to arrive at an agreement with the Soviet Union that might make it possible to diminish the scope of Western rearmament.

When, however, Edgar Faure presented his finance bill to the Assembly, a bill which provided for increased taxes, only the Socialists, most of the Popular Republicans, and about half of the Radicals—the members of his own party—supported him. He was defeated by a disparate majority, consisting of the RPF, almost all the Moderates, the other half of the Radicals, and the Com-

183

munists. Six weeks earlier the Assembly had refused, because of Socialist opposition, to accept the methods suggested by Premier René Pleven for effecting economies. Edgar Faure had succeeded in bringing the Socialists back into the majority, but at the same time he had alienated its conservative elements, the Moderates and the Radicals.

It looked as if the crisis would be long and difficult. At the beginning of March, Antoine Pinay, a Moderate deputy from Loire and for several years the Minister of Public Works in the Center cabinets, accepted the designation as Premier. There were few persons who believed it would be possible for him to receive the investiture of the Assembly, where it was believed he would be opposed by the Communists, Socialists, Gaullists, and the trade-union, socialistic group within the MRP. Pinay outlined a program calling for recourse to government borrowing and economy measures in order to balance the budget without increasing taxes, and he stated that it would be possible to reduce prices without resorting to a controlled economy. To everyone's surprise, Pinay was invested, thanks to a small number of defections in the MRP and, especially, to the favorable votes of twenty-seven rather conservative RPF deputies who rebelled against the instructions to maintain a systematic opposition—in their eyes, a *politique du pire*—given by General de Gaulle to his party.

For the first time in five years, the Radicals had voted unanimously to invest a Premier, in the belief that Pinay would not be invested and that their action would later be rewarded with Moderate support for a Radical candidate for the premiership. The split in the RPF thwarted this calculation. But the deed was committed and the Radicals had to suffer the consequences: they could not refuse to aid Pinay in applying a policy which, no doubt, they would have been much happier to see put into effect by a member of their own party.

Very quickly, control over the political situation slipped away from the parties and even, to a certain extent, from the parliamentary assemblies. Pinay's program—to reduce prices, to postpone certain expenditures, to stabilize tax rates, to restore the credit of the state in preparation for a loan to cover the investment and reconstruction program—created a great wave of hope in the country. As soon as it was known that there was no intention of increasing the tax burden, prices stopped rising and even, in some cases, declined slightly. With public confidence restored, purchases of treasury bonds increased considerably. The price of gold on the open market declined. Pinay had the good fortune to take office at the time when the break in the prices of certain raw materials on the world market gave his policy of lowering prices in a climate of economic liberalism maximum opportunity for success. But he also had the merit of being able to inspire confidence through the simplicity of his public statements and the firm will they revealed. Political circles were skeptical or reserved; many of the militants of the parties, especially of the MRP, did not hide their hostility to a policy which they regarded as too conservative. But the pressure of public opinion on the members of parliament was to provide the most effective support for the Pinay cabinet, whose composition was almost the same as that of its predecessors.

It is important to note in this regard that each time that he had to ask for a vote of confidence, Pinay asked that the vote be held on a Tuesday, *after* the weekly trip of the deputies to their constituencies, while his predecessors had almost always preferred that the vote be held on Friday, *before* the deputies visited their districts. The pressure of public opinion is capable of bringing to the Pinay government as many doubtful votes as it threatened to alienate from the earlier cabinets.

It was in these circumstances that Pinay, continually supported by a fraction of the RPF varying in size from thirty to fifty deputies, as well as by the Moderates, the Radicals, and the majority of the Popular Republicans, was able to enact before Easter a finance law which provided for no new taxes, imposed certain economies in nonmilitary expenses, and postponed a large portion of the expenditures for reconstruction and re-equipment until funds could be obtained to cover them through public borrowing. In the attempt to ensure the success of the proposed loan, he secured enactment of a fiscal amnesty applying to all past tax evasions, at the same time that the machinery for discovering future cases of tax evasion was strengthened and penalties for tax evasion were made more severe. The purpose of this amnesty was to make it possible to bring back into circulation hidden capital which, because its owners did not want to attract the attention of the tax collector, was until then placed in unrecorded investments or resting in sterile hoards.

In addition, the new government affirmed the continuity of French foreign policy by obtaining from the Council of the Republic the unqualified ratification of the treaty establishing the European Coal and Steel Community. The government itself signed, several weeks later, the contractual agreements with the Bonn Federal Republic and the treaty for the European Defense Community.

During the Easter parliamentary recess, elections were held for one-half of the seats in the Council of the Republic. The selection of senators is made by delegates chosen by the municipal councils which were elected in 1947, so no abrupt change in the balance of parties in the second chamber could occur. Nevertheless, the RPF lost several seats to the Moderates and especially to the MRP, which thereby partially avenged the electoral disaster it had suffered in November 1948 and proved that it was becoming more deeply rooted in the country.

At the end of May, Pinay won approval for a bond issue carrying a gold-based guarantee of its capital value as well as complete tax immunity, even from inheritance taxes. Then, confident of the success of his policy of reducing prices, he obtained the passage of a law establishing a sliding scale for the guaranteed minimum wage in the event of an increase of more than 5 per cent in the cost of living. It was specified, however, that the calculation of price movements would be made from the base date of December 1951, which precluded any immediate application of the sliding scale. This provision provoked the opposition of the Socialists and some members of the MRP and of the RPF, as well as of the Communists, toward the bill.

The unity of the Gaullist movement was seriously damaged by the opposition of the leaders of the RPF to Pinay's policies and by the support which almost one-third of the RPF deputies gave to Pinay. There is every reason to believe that this persistent tactical divergency will sooner or later produce a schism in the group, although until the present moment only three deputies, all of whom were Moderate deputies before the war, have officially left it.

As to the MRP, its congress at the end of May demonstrated that many of its militants, hostile to the fiscal amnesty for moral reasons and hardly pleased over the fiscal advantages conceded to the subscribers to the new bond issue, are especially afraid that the new budgetary policy will produce, because of the reduction of the investment and reconstruction program, economic and social retrogression. But the congress had to accept the continuation of Christian Democratic support of, and even participation in, the government, because it understood in doing so that it reflected the desires of the great majority of its voters, and therefore of its deputies.

In the purely political realm, in short, at the beginning of the summer it seems that the majority formed around the government of Antoine Pinay is not threatened with early disintegration.

The Significance of Pinay's Success

The Pinay majority, composed of a fraction of the RPF, of three-fourths of the MRP, and of all the liberals of the Moderate groups and the RGR, is precisely the one referred to in Chapter V as appearing, at the beginning of 1952, unlikely but nevertheless entirely conceivable if the strength of the organized parties were to be weakened by a return to an electoral system employing two ballots and the single-member district.

The question of changing the electoral system has not been

raised yet under the Pinay government. But everything indicates that the disintegration of the majority composed of the parties which were allied in one-third of the constituencies for the elections of June 1951 has made the maintenance of the present electoral system impossible. The re-establishment of single-member districts has been considered as a certainty as soon as the question should come before the Assembly. This prospect has been sufficient to encourage the independence of the RPF and MRP deputies from their parties and to inspire them with great consideration for the manifestations of public opinion in their constituencies. At the beginning of March, an impasse existed from which there seemed to be no exit: the Pleven cabinet had succumbed to the opposition of the Socialists; the Faure cabinet had succumbed to the opposition of the Moderates and the Radicals; the Socialists had refused even to take part in discussions at which representatives of the RPF would have been present, and General de Gaulle had restated his intention to practice a policy of systematic opposition as long as the "regime of parties" did not crumble.

But it was precisely the apparently insoluble nature of the crisis, due to the stubborn maintenance by the parties of their irreconcilable attitudes, which caused the weakening of their grip on public life by persuading part of the RPF, out of fear of a severe financial crisis with all its economic, social, and international consequences, to violate the instructions of General de Gaulle.

Once this movement of the politicians toward liberation from their parties got under way, the current of opinion which flowed through every social class after Pinay had launched his slogans calling for lower prices and the stabilization of taxes quickly became irresistible. The parties lost control over the direction of political action; left to their own devices they had led the country into an impasse.

This is what produced the strength of a government which the National Assembly could not reverse; the Assembly felt that public

opinion supported it. The failure of the Communist demonstrations against General Ridgway in May and then the failure of
the general strike called in protest against the arrest of Jacques
Duclos, the Communist leader, furnished proof that this popular
support included a large part of working-class opinion, undoubtedly that part of it which is more responsive to the demands
of thrifty housewives than to partisan slogans. It is significant that
in June 1952, in the election of the shop committee by the employees of the Régie Renault, the largest manufacturing plant in
the Paris area, the Communists lost the majority that they had
held for seven years, and that in the by-election of June 22 in the
second district of Seine, which embraces the wealthiest areas of
the capital, the RPF lost two-thirds of its votes of June 17, 1951.

The wave of confidence created by the advent to power of Antoine Pinay and by his first four months of governmental activity
clearly affects all the social groups of the nation and, whether
they like it or not, the parties are obliged to take it into consideration.

The Prospects for the Future

To say all this is certainly not to say that all of France's political
problems have been solved. The problem of institutional reform
remains, and it appears, unfortunately, that the new majority is
not entirely aware of its importance.

Economic and financial problems are equally troublesome. As
real as the decline in prices has been, it has been slight (from 2
to 3 per cent), and Pinay has regarded it as insufficient. He thinks
that industrial prices still include too many vestiges of the wide
margins that were imposed during recent years as insurance against
inflation, and he has repeated more than once that if these margins do not disappear his government will be forced to reintroduce
price control. A Moderate cabinet, despairing of the effectiveness
of liberal economic methods and of the good will of businessmen,
would then find itself applying the economic program of the Socialists and the left-wing, socialistic fraction of the MRP. In this

case, however, would it be able to retain the support of the majority that rallied around it in the spring?

In addition, it does not seem certain that the loan floated in June will bring in enough resources to permit, in 1952, the complete unfreezing of the funds for investment and reconstruction initially envisaged in the budget. If these resources continue to be inadequate, will it be possible to continue to avoid taxation and resort exclusively to borrowing in order to finance capital expenditures? In any event, the preparation of the 1953 budget will require some difficult decisions. It would be dangerous to slacken the investment program, which involves the reconstruction and the modernization of the productive facilities of the country. An increase in existing tax rates being precluded, as well as, undoubtedly, another sizable bond issue, the only possibility would be a reform of the very structure of the French tax system. By way of preparation, the Pinay government has appointed a committee of experts whose conclusions will certainly be submitted to Parliament with next year's budget. But in order to increase revenue without increasing the tax rates, any fiscal reform must reduce the possibilities for tax evasion and enlarge the area of application of existing taxes. In other words, it should strike at the fiscal privileges, which the farmers and owners of small businesses now enjoy and which are certainly economically undesirable because such privileges contribute to the survival of unproductive enterprises.

Table 4 classifies taxpayers according to source of income. It shows the preponderance of taxable income to be in the form of salaries and wages, which certainly does not correspond to the existing situation; for while salaries and wages must be reported by the persons paying them, the table reflects the legal privileges of the farmers, the owners of small businesses, and the professional people, whose taxes are calculated on the basis of income tables rather than actual income. It is among these social groups that the Moderates and Radicals seem to find most of their electoral support. Will these parties agree, in order to preserve their present political influence, to impose sacrifices upon their own supporters?

Table 4. Number of taxpayers with incomes of more than 1,000,000 francs.

Net Taxable Income	Industrial and Commercial Profits	Agricultural Profits	Professional Income	Salaries and Wages
1,000,000 to				
2,500,000 francs	31,503	4,646	15,443	62,458
2,500,000 to				
5,000,000 francs	6,815	1,215	3,943	12,374
More than				
5,000,000 francs	1,750	549	1,742	3,970
Totals	40,068	6,410	21,128	78,802

Obviously, this question cannot be answered at the present moment. Perhaps a government of the Right Center, not arousing *a priori* hostility among the people who now enjoy tax privileges, would be best situated politically to carry out a genuine fiscal reform. In any case, it must be recognized that these problems exist, and that the final result of the political experiment undertaken by Pinay, who prefers to speak of a "policy of experience," will depend in the last analysis upon the extent to which its advocates will understand and accept the economic and fiscal conditions for its success.

As to the national oposition parties—the members of the RPF faithful to the orders of General de Gaulle, the Socialist Party, and the left wing of the MRP—it should simply be said in concluding that they have not yet shown the slightest desire to pave the way for the *rapprochement* which the author persists in believing would be fruitful, but which he fears will be impossible to create for a long time, due to the mutually contradictory intransigence of General de Gaulle and the Socialist and Christian Democratic leaders.

Index

Action Française, 148
Alain, on democracy, 153-154, 157
Assembly of the French Union, x-xi
Association of capital and labor, 49-50, 139, 170
Atlantic Pact, 51, 86, 89, 176
Auriol, Vincent, 38, 131, 132
elected President of the Republic, 20-21

Barangé, Charles, 133-134, 174
Barrachin, Edmond, 133-134
Bidault, Georges, x, 1, 12, 16, 18, 25, 43, 67
Blum, Léon, 3-4, 7, 18-19, 21, 29, 35, 36, 39, 41
Boulet, Paul, 89

Cabinet, its relations with National Assembly, x, 164-166
Capitant, René, 54, 55
Catholic schools, 40-41, 46, 83
background of problem of, 124-129
in 1951 election campaign, 87
problem of before new National Assembly, 123-124, 129-136
public attitudes toward, 91-92
CFTC, see French Confederation of Christian Workers
CGT, see General Confederation of Labor
Christian Democracy, see Mouvement Républicain Populaire
Clemenceau, Michel, candidate for presidency, 20

Collective bargaining, restoration of, 43
Cominform (Information Bureau of the Communist and Workers' parties), 31
Committee of National Liberation, composition of, 5-6
Communist party, 157-158, 162
activities during occupation, 4-5
beginning of decline, 11
and Catholic schools, 41, 126, 134
and constitution, 9, 159
and economic policy, 22-23
and foreign policy, 25, 31, 37, 47
and De Gaulle, 4, 6-7, 26
and Indo-China, 22-25
isolation of, 80, 173
ministers removed from cabinet, 24-25
and municipal elections, 32
and national elections:
comparison between 1936 and 1945, 5
distribution of combined Communist and other extreme Left vote in June 1951, 114
geographical and social analysis of results of June 1951, 95-100
parliamentary strength of, 118
parliamentary tactics of, 45, 65, 67, 139
and strikes, 15, 24, 37, 42, 47
and union elections, 189
Constitution:

Constitution (*continued*)
 criticism of, 159-161, 164-166
 modified in practice, x-xi
 revision agreed upon, 46
 revision not undertaken, 73
Council of the Republic, x-xi
 conflicts with National Assembly, 46
 elections for, 186
 electoral law for, 45-46, 65
Cudenet, Gabriel, opposes dissolution, 53

Daladier, Edouard, 4, 19-20, 85-86
Decree-laws, 139, 169
Democracy:
 and communism, 157-159
 definition of, 148
 and economic structure, 154-155
 French conception of, 152-154
 French opposition to, 148-152, 155
 need for extension to economic sphere, 170-171
 and Rassemblement du Peuple Français, 149
 and religion, 150-152, 159-160
 and socialism, 156-157
Duclos, Jacques, 189

Economic Council, x-xi
Elections:
 cantonal, 42, 63
 of Council of the Republic (1951), 186
 municipal, 31-32
 national, of June 2, 1946, 11-12
 national, of November 10, 1946, 17
 national, of June 17, 1951:
  abstentions, 93-94
  analysis of results by alliances, 110-117
  analysis of results in terms of economic structure, 111-117, 142
  campaign and alliances, 80-89
  general analysis of over-all results, 91-93
  geographical and social analysis of results for each party:
   Communist party, 95-100
   Moderate parties, 102-104

   Mouvement Républicain Populaire, 106-108
   Rassemblement des Gauches Républicaines, 103-106
   Rassemblement du Peuple Français, 100-102
   Socialist party, 108-110
  results compared with 1946, 90
Electoral alliances:
 geographical distribution of, 81-85
 none made by Communist party, 80
 of Rassemblement du Peuple Français, 56-57, 80, 82-83
 results of June 1951 elections in terms of, 110-117
Electoral system:
 for cantonal elections, 63
 for election of Council of the Republic, 45-46, 65-66
 for municipal elections, 30, 64
 for national elections in 1945 and 1946, 58-59, 74
 for national elections in 1951 (law of May 9, 1951), 74-78, 161-163
 attitude toward:
  of Moderates, 63, 69, 72, 139
  of Mouvement Républicain Populaire, 37, 44, 64, 69-72, 139
  of Radicals, 44, 60, 62-63, 73-74, 139
  of Rassemblement du Peuple Français, 64-65, 68, 73, 139
  of Socialists, 64, 139
 Coty system, 70
 majority list system, 61, 65, 69, 163-164
 majority system with one ballot not considered, 68
 Roques-Tailhade system, 71-72, 75
 single-member district system, 65, 69-70, 77, 163, 174
 revival of deemed certain, 188
 two-ballot system, 44, 68-69, 77, 163-164
 see also Proportional representation
European Defense Community, 183, 186

Falloux law, 127
Fascism, 149
Faure, Edgar, 85, 182, 183-184, 188

Ferry, Jules, and educational system, 123, 125, 126
First Constituent Assembly, composition of, 8
Force Ouvrière, 40, 50
Foreign policy, agreement of non-Communist parties on, 86-87
Fourth Force, 86-87
French Confederation of Christian Workers (CFTC), 50
French Union, 119, 144

Gardey, Abel, 82
Gasser, Jules, candidate for presidency, 20
Gaulle, Charles de, 47ff., 161, 176
    announces program for association of capital and labor, 49
    and Communist party, 4, 6-7, 26
    and constitution, 12-13, 16
    creates Rassemblement du Peuple Français, 26-28
    demands new electoral law and dissolution of National Assembly, 37
    and Moderates, 52
    and "national unanimity," 6, 137
    and Mouvement Républicain Populaire, 3, 8-9, 12-14, 28
    and Radicals, 6, 52
    and Rassemblement des Gauches Républicaines, 53-54
    resignation of, 7-9
    see also Rassemblement du Peuple Français
Gaullism, see Rassemblement du Peuple Français
Gaullist Union, 17-18
General Confederation of Labor (CGT), 15, 22, 24, 38, 50
    schism in, 40
Giacobbi, Paul, 54
    suggests an electoral system, 70-71
Gouin, Félix, and tripartism, 8-9

Herriot, Edouard, 20, 85, 86, 106, 136, 179
Ho Chi Minh, see Indo-China

Independent Republican Group, see Moderate parties

Indo-China, problem of policy in, 21-23

Jouvenel, Robert de, 141, 154

Korean War:
    effects of on parties, 43, 121
    and armament effort, 144

La Chambre, Guy, 83
Le Corre, Darius, 111

Marie, André, forms short-lived government, 41
Maroselli, André, 82
Marshall Plan:
    aids economic recovery, xiii, 45
    opposed by Communists, 31, 37
Masson, Jean, 54
Maurras, Charles, 149-150
Mayer, Daniel, 15, 39
Mayer, René, 39, 43, 131-132
    and Catholic schools, 131
    withdraws 5,000-franc notes from circulation, 42n.
Menthon, François de, 10
Moch, Jules, 43
Moderate parties:
    and Catholic schools, 87, 107, 123, 130, 134
    and constitution, 138-139, 160
    discredited after Liberation, 2
    and economic policy, 36, 41-42, 121-122, 135, 139, 172, 189
    and electoral system, 63, 69, 72, 139
    and Indo-China, 22-23
    and municipal elections, 31-32
    and 1951 national election results, 102-104
    parliamentary strength of, 119
    and Rassemblement du Peuple Français, 28-32, 36, 38, 49-57, 85, 174-175, 180
    reorganization of, 86-87
    tactics of, 19-20, 29-30, 42
Mollet, Guy, 15, 33-34, 35
Monnet Plan, xiii, 143-144, 146
Montel, Pierre, 54
Moscow Conference, effects of on attitude of French Communist party, 25

Moulin, Jean, 5-6
Moutet, Marius, and policy in Indo-China, 22
Mouvement Républicain Populaire (MRP):
  aims of, 12, 13, 28
  and Catholic schools, 40-41, 87, 107, 123, 130-131, 134-135
  and Communist party, 14, 17, 19, 21, 45
  and constitution, 9-10, 14, 16, 46, 138-139, 160
  and De Gaulle, 3, 8-9, 12-14, 28
  and economic policy, 45, 121-122, 135, 139, 172
  and electoral system, 37, 44, 64, 69-72, 139
  immediate postwar position of, 3
  and Indo-China, 22-23
  membership of, 162
  and municipal elections, 32, 106
  and 1951 national election results, 106-108
  parliamentary strength of, 119
  and Pinay government, 185, 187, 188
  and Rassemblement du Peuple Français, 27-28, 37, 48, 50, 53, 55, 86, 179-181, 191
  and Socialist party, 8, 12, 14, 28, 41, 50
  and Vatican, 89
MRP, *see* Mouvement Républicain Populaire

National Assembly:
  First National Assembly adjourns, 80
  First National Assembly in conflict with Council of the Republic, 46
  Second National Assembly:
    strength of parties in, 117-120
    various majorities in, 138, 173, 176
  procedure in, 161, 166-169
  relations with cabinet, x, 164-166
National Council of the Resistance, composition of, 6
Nationalization, aim of, 170
Neutralists, 89, 111

L'Osservatore Romano, 89

Paul-Boncour, J., 124, 129, 130
Peasant party, *see* Moderate parties
Pétainistes, 88, 102, 149
Petsche, Maurice, 42, 43, 82, 132
Philip, André, 30, 34
Pierre, Abbé, 89
Pinay, Antoine, xi, 84
  composition of majority supporting his government, 187
  economic policy of, 184-187, 189-191
  formation of government by, 183-184
  popular support of, 185, 188-189
Pineau, Christian, 41, 42
Pleven, René, x, 43-44, 53, 54, 73, 84, 85, 135, 171, 181, 184, 188
  and Catholic schools, 123, 132
  criticizes Rassemblement du Peuple Français, 55
Poincaré, Raymond, on parliamentary committee system, 166n.
Poinso-Chapuis, Germaine, 41, 123
Popular Front, 150
President of the Republic, election of, 20-21
Private schools, *see* Catholic schools
PRL (Republican Party of Liberty), *see* Moderate parties
Proportional representation:
  adopted in 1945 and 1946, 58
  in the Coty system, 70
  in the law of May 9, 1951, 74-76, 162
  in municipal elections, 32
  postwar attitudes toward:
    of Moderate parties, 63
    of Mouvement Républicain Populaire, 37, 64, 70
    of Radicals, 62-63, 66
    of Rassemblement du Peuple Français, 64, 68
    of Socialist party, 64
  prewar attitudes toward:
    of Catholic conservatives, 59
    of Communists, 60
    of Socialists, 60
    of Radicals, 60
  reasons for adoption of, 59-62
  reasons for abandonment of, 66-67

in the Roques-Tailhade system, 71-72

see also Electoral system

Queuille, Henri, 42, 43, 44, 84, 93, 119, 130
  asks early adjournment of National Assembly, 80
  persuades Parliament to pass new electoral law, 73-74

Radical-Socialist party:
  and Catholic schools, 41, 62, 86, 87, 106, 124, 126, 130, 134
  and constitution, 138-139, 160
  and economic policy, 36, 62, 121-122, 135, 139, 179
  and electoral system, 44, 60, 62-63, 73-74, 139
  and Indo-China, 22-23
  membership of, 162
  and municipal elections, 32
  and 1951 national election results, 103-106
  and Rassemblement du Peuple Français, 28-29, 36, 38, 49-57, 85, 174, 179-180
  tactics of, 19-20, 29-31, 184
  see also Rassemblement des Gauches Républicaines

Ramadier, Paul, 21, 23, 29, 31-35

Rassemblement des Gauches Républicaines (RGR):
  and Catholic schools, 87, 91-92, 134
  composition of, 11-12
  divergence within, 86, 88
  and economic policy, 30, 36, 41-42, 121-122
  and municipal elections, 31-32
  and 1951 national election results, 103-106
  parliamentary strength of, 119
  and Rassemblement du Peuple Français, 28-32, 36, 49-57, 85-86
  tactics of, 29-30

Rassemblement du Peuple Français (RPF), 49-57, 149, 162
  and Catholic schools, 87, 107, 123, 130, 134-135
  and constitution, 51, 139, 177
  creation of, 26-28

  and economic policy, 122, 135, 139, 177-178
  and electoral alliances, 56-57, 100
  and electoral system, 64-65, 68, 73, 139
  and foreign policy, 86, 178
  intergroup organized by, 31
  and municipal elections, 31-32
  and 1951 national election results, 100-102
    distribution of combined Rassemblement du Peuple Français and allied vote in June 1951, 112
  loses badly in by-election in June 1952, 189
  parliamentary strength of, 118
  schism in, 184, 187-188
  tactics of, 50-51, 53, 135, 174-175, 177, 181, 188
  see also De Gaulle

Referendums:
  of May 5, 1946, 10-11, 160
  of October 13, 1946, 16-17

Republican Party of Liberty (PRL), *see* Moderate parties

Resistance:
  effects on postwar politics, 2-6
  as basis for new coalition, 180

Revolution of 1789, effects on subsequent political developments, 140-141, 150-151

Reynaud, Paul, 4, 34-35, 39, 41, 42, 43, 53, 82

RGR, *see* Rassemblement des Gauches Républicaines

Ribes, Champetier de, candidate for presidency, 20

Right, *see* Moderate parties

Roques, Raymond, proposal of for electoral system, 71-72, 75

RPF, *see* Rassemblement du Peuple Français

Schuman Plan, 171-172, 177, 186

Schuman, Robert, 38-39, 41-42, 53, 84

Second Constituent Assembly, composition of, 11-12

Second Empire, economic developments during, 141, 143

Senate, stronghold of conservatism, 10

Siegfried, André, on French conception of democracy, 153
Socialist party, 156-157, 162
and Catholic schools, 40-41, 87, 124, 126, 130, 134-135
and Communist party, 15-16, 18, 19, 23, 29, 31, 33, 45, 159, 173
and constitution, 9, 138-139, 159
and economic policy, 21-22, 29, 33, 43, 44-45, 87, 121-122, 129, 135, 139, 172-173
and electoral system, 6, 64, 139
favors continuance of Ramadier government, 28-30
immediate postwar position of, 3-4
and Indo-China, 22-23, 29
Lyons congress of, 15-16
ministers of leave government, 43
and Mouvement Républicain Populaire, 33, 41
and municipal elections, 32
and 1951 national election results, 108-110
parliamentary strength of, 119
provokes almost all ministerial crises, 44-45
and Rassemblement du Peuple Français, 26-27, 29-30, 33, 37, 45, 48, 50, 53, 85, 179-181, 191
Soustelle, Jacques, 55
Strikes, 24, 37-38, 40, 42

Tailhade, Clément, proposal of for electoral system, 71-72, 75
Tanguy-Prigent, François Marie, 34
Taxation, 45, 46, 80, 88, 183, 185, 186, 190-191
Teitgen, Pierre Henri, 83
Third Force:
conception of, 33-34
failure to find majority support for, 36
Third International:
dissolution of, 6
reappears camouflaged as Cominform, 31
Third Republic, ix, xii, xiii, 138
and Catholic schools, 125
economic characteristics of, 141-142, 153
Thomson, David, on French conception of democracy, 152-153
Thorez, Maurice, candidate for premiership, 18
Titoism, 111
Tripartism, 1-2, 9-24

UDSR, *see* Union Démocratique et Socialiste de la Résistance
Union Démocratique et Socialiste de la Résistance (UDSR):
composition of, 12
prohibits its members from joining Rassemblement du Peuple Français, 54
see also Rassemblement des Gauches Républicaines

Varenne, Alexander, 1
Vatican:
and Catholic schools, 123
organ of favors Mouvement Républicain Populaire, 89
Vichy government, 5, 11, 98
and Catholic schools, 124, 125
nostalgia for, 149
Viet Minh, *see* Indo-China
Voting, best time for, 79-80
see also Electoral system, Proportional representation